PRAISE FOR *PERFECT SELLING*

The 5-Step process in this book is one of the most closely aligned to a successful sales interaction that I have encountered. I believe the advice given by Linda is practical and very useable by a salesperson on a day-to-day basis. If salespeople follow this 5-Step process, they will become top sales performers within the companies in which they work.

Malcolm Rees
Global Head of Sales
DHL Express

Imagine a travel genie that already knows where you want to go before you climb onto the magic carpet. Linda Richardson's *Perfect Selling* will help you build your own internal genie to navigate every call, keep your focus on your customer, and maximize the success of every sales call.

Ken Daly
CEO
National Association of Corporate Directors

I can't think of anyone better to author *Perfect Selling* than the world's most perfect seller. You will want to jump up and start banging on doors once you learn the 5 Steps and secrets of Linda's science of selling.

Pat Croce
Best-selling motivational books author
and serial entrepreneur

Perfect Selling is about using everything you've got, heightening your awareness, and developing your talent. That's magic and it is thrilling.

Gerhard Gschwandtner
Founder and Publisher
Selling Power

Perfect Selling provides tangible components and a set of disciplines that is adaptable and versatile and leads to results.

James Jacobson
Vice President of Sales
EchoStar

Linda Richardson's other books on selling cover masterfully all the many elements of a successful sale. This one goes for the center of the target—*the sales call itself.* That moment of truth when the curtain goes up and the spotlights come on, and all the many hours of careful preparation and planning can either pay off big time or be irretrievably lost. A must-read for anyone serious about professional selling.

Michael S. Kaye
Managing Partner
ClearLight Partners

PERFECT
SELLING

OPEN THE DOOR. CLOSE THE DEAL.

Linda Richardson
Bestselling Author of *Stop Telling, Start Selling*

New York   Chicago   San Francisco   Lisbon   London
Madrid   Mexico City   Milan   New Delhi   San Juan   Seoul
Singapore   Sydney   Toronto

1 2 3 4 5 6 7 8 9 0   DOC/DOC   0 9 8

ISBN: 978-0-07-154989-9
MHID: 0-07-154989-7

This publication is designed to provide accurate and authoritative information in regard to the subject matter covered. It is sold with the understanding that the publisher is not engaged in rendering legal, accounting, or other professional service. If legal advice or other expert assistance is required, the services of a competent professional person should be sought.

> —*From a declaration of principles jointly adopted by a committee of the American Bar Association and a committee of publishers.*

McGraw-Hill books are available at special quantity discounts to use as premiums and sales promotions, or for use in corporate training programs. To contact a representative please visit the Contact Us pages at www.mhprofessional.com.

Library of Congress Cataloging-in-Publication Data

Richardson, Linda.
    Perfect selling : open the door. close the deal. / by Linda Richardson.
        p. cm.
    Includes bibliographical references and index.
    ISBN 0-07-154989-7 (alk. paper)
1. Selling.   2. Interpersonal communication.   I. Title.
  HF5438.25.R5127 2008
  658.85—dc22

                                                2008008061

For
Emily and Dylan,
perfection times two

CONTENTS

"Speak as common
    people do, but think
        as wise men do."

—ARISTOTLE

FOREWORD

We all love walking along the banks of a river. Sometimes we see a lone rower break the still surface with his blades, body, and boat synchronized. Rowers say that it takes a lifetime to achieve one perfect stroke.

Think of how many sales calls you have made in your career. Can you pick out one where everything was **perfect**? If you can't think of one, then you haven't been selling long enough, or your company hasn't trained you well enough.

Like Linda Richardson, I have been selling for over 30 years. I have trained over 10,000 salespeople in Europe and the United States and published 18 books on the subject. I've experienced some of the most thrilling sales possible in my career and it never ceases to amaze me how easy and effortless selling can be if you do right. How? Linda's book will show you the path.

Mary Kay Ash once told me, "Most people die with their music still unplayed." I believe we're all born with an instrument inside. For some it is the piano, for others a set of drums, for others the clarinet. It is our job to find the instrument we're most suited for and then learn how to play it better than anyone else.

Many people ask, "Are salespeople born, or made?" It is an unproductive question. We're all born, and we're all formed by a multitude of forces that shape us into who we are at the present moment. A more productive question would be, "How can I become the top in my field with the talents I've got?" The salesperson with little talent, but with a fervent desire to be the best he or she can be, has a far greater chance of becoming successful than a highly talented, but unmotivated, salesperson. Many people say, "If I were more talented, I'd spend more time developing my talents." These are the people Mary Kay talked about; they are destined to die with their music still unplayed.

Think back to the rower. You can't row a boat with only one oar in the water. One oar is the talent you develop through ongoing training; the other oar is who you are as a person. Both oars need to be in synch to move forward if you want to win in selling.

Perfect Selling is about using everything you've got. It will heighten your awareness when you are in the sales call. It will develop your talent, help you create new customers, and strengthen relationships—and that's perfect. That's magic, and it is thrilling.

— **GERHARD GSCHWANDTNER**
Founder and Publisher of *Selling Power*

INTRODUCTION

In July 2006, when Linda Richardson asked me to assume the role of President and CEO of Richardson, I gratefully accepted. I had grown with the company and was passionate about our business. I joined Richardson in 1992 as CFO and, after more than a decade in that role, became EVP with client relationship responsibilities. As I began this new role, I remember meeting with Linda and her telling me she thought I had everything—natural talent, strong technical background, solid strategic sense, experience, drive, and true "likeability." She offered me the chance to work with her on a final essential ingredient—mastering the actual sales call.

My ego spiked. Prior to coming to Richardson, I had been a CPA for more than a decade. What did she think I was doing all those years—to say nothing of my 14 years with Richardson? Detecting that I wasn't very receptive, Linda let the topic go.

My initial client meetings went well but I knew I wasn't making the progress I expected. It was at this point that I realized my natural ability and experience were not giving me all it takes to win.

Feedback is a way of life at Richardson so I went to my "coach." Linda and I focused on a large opportunity I was working on. I had already done my client and industry homework. I knew our offerings cold. Over a few days, we worked on understanding the structure of the sales call while, at the same time, we prepared for this big call. As I think back, the toughest hurdle wasn't being able to understand what to do in the call—it was the "aha" of realizing I had so much to learn despite all my experience.

By the day of my call, I had it laid out like a map. I was ready in a way I had never been before. During the call, I felt a little like I was directing a movie. In fact, I was coaching myself. I knew where I wanted to go and I got there. That call led to a deal we consider "historic" for our 30-year history.

A believer—yes. But more importantly, like Linda, I know we are all born with natural gifts that we bring to the table. I also know that those gifts deserve honing. *Perfect Selling* is the way to perfect your sales calls. Each page, each lesson is a path to sales excellence. The best part is the awareness and confidence you will gain. After reading *Perfect Selling* you will be your own coach, and your learning never stops.

— **DAVID DISTEFANO**

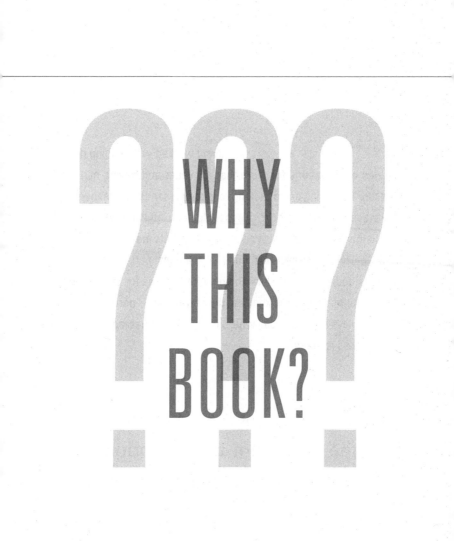

WHY THIS BOOK?

Having worked with leading global sales organizations for more than 25 years and having had the pleasure of training and coaching tens of thousands of salespeople, I have seen the world's best salespeople bring intelligence and passion to their jobs. I have also seen what prevents many salespeople from "perfect" selling. This book is the culmination of several decades dedicated to understanding what it takes for salespeople to walk out of a sales call knowing they have had a "perfect call"—not a flawless call, but a call where they have connected and know the business is theirs.

Perfect Selling can be
the norm, not the exception
for sales professionals who yearn
to be the best they can be.

"At the end of the day,
it is the salesperson
and the customer
'in the moment'
where the sale is made."

—JOHN REED
Former Chairman, Citibank

Anyone in sales realizes it takes talent and effort to succeed as a salesperson. There is no doubt that marketing, sales strategy, preparation, technical expertise, business knowledge, keeping pace with technology, fast access to accurate information, and drive, along with the ability to leverage the team and tap into resources, are all critical factors to succeed in sales today. *But I believe nothing can have **a greater and faster impact** on increasing your sales results than improving what happens when you and your customer are "in the moment" in the call.*

**When all is said and done
— and lost or won —**

**what happens in
the sales call matters.**

It is the quality of the time you spend in dialogue with your customer that can make or break the deal. For that is when your knowledge, experience, preparation, resources, business acumen, and sales strategy all come together to make it happen.

The dialogue during a sales call is not ordinary conversation. The difference between ordinary conversation and sales dialogue is that a conversation is casual. Conversation does and should meander. Sales dialogue must have direction. And to be success-ful in sales you must guide that direction.

Sales call time is precious. When you are with your cus-tomers you have a choice about how you use that time. You can have a clear plan that drives what you do and say during the call or you can let the situation and environment drive it. There really isn't an in-between. You can drive the sales call or let the sales call drive you. This doesn't mean you dominate the call. And of course it doesn't mean you don't adapt to the environment. Your dialogue can be natural and flexible and at the same time planned and controlled. You can "go with the flow" as long as you are headed in the right direction.

FIVE STEPS

When you walk into a customer's office your adrenalin is up and there is a level of natural tension. As the sales call starts you are required to do two things: direct the flow of the call and engage in the dialogue. I have watched salespeople struggle with this. I have seen how hard it is for most of them to both direct and engage in dialogue when talking to their customers.

When Aristotle said, *"Speak as common people do, but think as wise men do,"* he separated thinking from talking. In a sense that is what I have done in this book. Recognizing that one influences the other, I have separated call direction from call dialogue. Focusing on direction, I have taken the sales call apart and broken it into 5 Steps. By making the 5 Steps of the call second-nature, you can free yourself to maximize every second of your sales call dialogue. By not having to figure out the steps, you can put all of your energies into hearing your customers and responding in a way that adds value and is as persuasive as possible.

The 5 Steps serve as a topographical map of the landscape of the sales call. By understanding the lay of the land, you will be clear about the direction you want your dialogue to take and you can focus your attention on the dialogue to get you there.

Most salespeople have a lot going for them—they have competitive products or their companies more than likely wouldn't be in business. For the most part they are in sales because they like being in the driver's seat and solving problems. They are articulate. They are personable. They like to compete and win. And they know their products.

But salespeople with strong technical knowledge who are fully prepared can still flounder. There are many talented and successful salespeople who are achieving under their real capability. A critical difference is the knowledge of the sales call. Even though the sales call is the place where salespeople spend the majority of their time, many don't understand its inner workings.

The one thing I have observed consistently with top performers is that they do know the terrain of the sales call. **Top performers**, in fact, have an intimate knowledge of the structure of the call whether that knowledge is on a conscious or subconscious level.

> They know where they are,
>> where they are going,
>>> and what they want to accomplish
>>>> every minute.

Their call structure, if you look under the dialogue, is consistent. They have a process and plan they follow to the tee—unless they deliberately decide to deviate from it.

"This is the greatest toy ever invented."

—CHARLIE CHAPLIN
(pointing to his temple)

"G.P.S."

Understanding the 5 Steps is like having a navigation device in your head during the sales call that is continuously pointing you in the right direction. The workings of a G.P.S. system are incredible, but they pale in comparison to the capabilities of the human mind.

As with a G.P.S., you are not on automatic pilot. You are not on cruise control. You do the driving (the talking), but you are pointed in the right direction so you don't get lost and you arrive where you want to be. Like any good G.P.S., when the situation requires it, you have alternate routes to lead you to your end destination, and you always have the option not to heed it based on other factors.

While the direction is set, the execution is entirely up to you. If you think about your body, the reason you don't fall is that your body has a sophisticated balance system in place. Every joint has proprioceptors that sense what is needed and make corrections, and this happens all under the radar without you realizing it. In the same way, knowing the sales call intimately at a gut level keeps you steady and on track. You are your own coach during the call. As I have coached tens of thousands of salespeople in seminars and from the sidelines, many have said they wish I could be with them on their sales calls to guide them and keep them going in the right direction. The 5 Steps let you become that coach for yourself. When you internalize the 5 Steps, your inner dialogue directs the dialogue you have with your customers.

I have seen a wide variety of salespeople—from sales stars to salespeople that managers had all but written off. But I have rarely seen a case where the combination of smarts, process, and drive failed to bring success. The number of salespeople who bomb despite these factors is few and far between. My decades of experience tell me, without question, that almost all salespeople can make perfect selling the rule, not the exception—but they need to know the ins and outs of the steps of the sales call.

The 5 Steps are:

- Connect

- Explore

- Leverage

- Resolve

- Act

These steps, or something like them, may be familiar to you. Unfortunately, the point isn't whether or not they are familiar. The important thing is how *expertly* you execute them. There are many good salespeople out there. There are a good number of very good salespeople. But there are very few superb salespeople. Most salespeople have their share of good calls but not enough "perfect" calls—where they consistently connect and win.

Just as you have technical knowledge in your head you can draw from when you walk into your customer's office or speak to your customer on the phone, by being able to summon up the 5 Steps because they are second-nature, you will have the information you need to drive the call toward your objective.

I've opened up each step of the call so there is no question how to maximize each moment with your customer. If at first it seems mechanical, in a way it is. But in much more important ways it is not. This is not a recipe book. This is not a script. This is about form, not formula. The difference is immense. Form gives you a way to drive the call so you are free to create the best dialogue. In a sales call you have to make decisions about where to go and what to say next quickly, and often under pressure. The key is to be able to make wise but fast decisions. You will be on solid ground even when a customer throws a curve ball. The steps give you the basis to improvise and come back remaining composed and in control.

HOW TO USE THIS BOOK

As Albert Einstein once said, "Everything should be made as simple as possible, but not more so." I have tried to do that in this book. The 5 Steps are simple to understand. Within each Step there are a few specific actions for you to accomplish—not every time but most of the time. The actions are really a discipline, not as in a "marching order" but in the true definition of discipline, learning. Some salespeople seem to be born knowing this discipline, but most of us—by working at it—can become not only proficient but superb. The easy part of this book is learning the steps and actions at an intellectual level. This comes first. A 20-minute effort will help you begin to internalize each of the 5 Steps so they are yours to turn on as you need them.

I suggest a **5-day program**—one step each day (or week)—a Monday through Friday sequence based on your expertise in sales and what works for you. By focusing on one step at a time before moving on to the next, you will go from understanding to doing, and experience the exponential power of incremental, one-step-at-a-time growth. Once you have "gotten" a step, apply it in several calls. You'll know when it is time to move to the next step, based on debriefing the day. But of course your plan is up to you. Drop in this book wherever and whenever you like, based on your needs.

I've included QuickPlanners and QuickDebriefs as tools to help you reinforce the Steps as you prepare, assess your skills, and self-coach every day. To access online versions of these *Perfect Selling* tools throughout the book, please go to http://www.richardson.com/Resource-Center/Perfect-Selling-Tools/ and enter Username: perfectseller and Password: Richardson.

The thing I wait for most from the new salespeople on our sales team at Richardson is the day they say to me, "It is too easy." That doesn't mean they don't work very hard every day or that they don't sell to demanding customers or against formidable competitors in every deal. It means they have gotten "it" and use "it" to close. You can, too.

I know firsthand that sales stars are made and not born. Sure there are naturals who intuitively know what it takes to win, but most of us can benefit from having a map for where we are going.

If your goal is to be your absolute best at sales, to enjoy the elation that comes with walking out of a call knowing it was "perfect," closing more business, and building stronger relationships, then become a master of the sales call—

take

the

first

STEP.

PERFECT SELLING

ONE

CONNECT

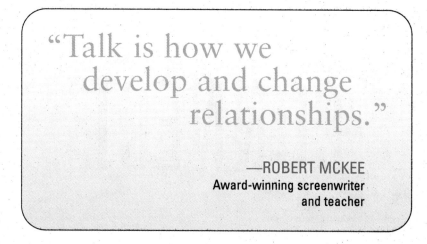

"Talk is how we develop and change relationships."

—ROBERT MCKEE
Award-winning screenwriter
and teacher

Think about your last sales call. How much attention did you pay to how you would begin that call? Probably not much. You probably focused on the real business of the call—what happens after the opening.

But your opening is real business. It can be the most human part of the call. It can be the most personal. It can be the most awkward and uncomfortable. It can also be the most gracious and fun. It can be many of these things at once. It is always telling. It is also your customer's window into you—

your style,

your professionalism,

your level of preparedness,

who you are—

and it gives you a good peek into the customer—if you look.

It is where you connect and set the stage for what will follow.

3

MUCH TO DO IN THE OPENING AND LITTLE TIME TO DO IT

Are you exactly sure how you will open when you start a sales call? There is real work to do—quickly. Quickly does not mean you gallop through the call. It means you have a very clear picture of the path you'll take to set the stage to maximize what follows.

This is the time to connect by building rapport, previewing the contents of the call, setting the tone, and reading and being read by your customer. How you use this time sends a clear message about you and what the customer can expect from the rest of the call. Unfortunately, too many salespeople go through the opening (and other parts of the sales dialogue) with little rhyme or reason. They let the opening take its own course and end when it does versus accomplishing the few key things that need to be done to start the call on the best foot possible.

Because there is a lot to do and not much time to do it, the clearer you are about what needs to be done, the better. Once you are sure of what you want to do in the opening, the dialogue to do it flows more easily.

When the call starts, be in the driver's seat.

Connecting is the first step of the call. It requires **4 Actions**. An Action is a discipline you follow. It is a behavior and the reaction from the customer you get to that behavior, i.e., you greet the customer and he or she greets you. You can complete the 4 Actions in Step 1 (with the exception of the time for rapport, which is the big variable) in a matter of a few minutes.

It may seem like too much to get through. But in fact you move very quickly through this stage of the call. These 4 Actions meld into each other, all in a few sentences. As a result you are perfectly poised for Step 2, Explore.

Once you try these actions, you'll see they flow like the ABCs. It is a relief because you know exactly what you want to accomplish without being robotic.

> **Your message,**
>
>> **your words,**
>>
>>> **and your delivery**
>>>
>>>> **are** entirely your own

and therefore the dialogue is natural, as is the conscious decision to deviate from any of the Actions if necessary—but you know how you want to use this important time to make the best possible connection. As the situation requires, you make whatever adjustments are needed. For example, if you learn your customer has a time constraint you may forgo rapport. Although the Actions point your dialogue in a direction, you are guided by the Actions, not locked in by them.

Let's focus on the 4 Actions.

☐ **ACTION 1:** Greet/High-Mileage Rapport

☐ **ACTION 2:** Summary of Events/
Leverage Preparation

☐ **ACTION 3:** Dual Purpose and Check

☐ **ACTION 4:** Transition to Needs

ACTION 1: Greet/High-Mileage Rapport

Greet

Of course you know how to say hello and introduce yourself. But as Malcolm Gladwell's best-selling book *Blink: The Power of Thinking Without Thinking* makes clear, people communicate more than they realize in "the blink of an eye." In the first few seconds both you and your customer send cues and make judgments. The impression you make can be positive or negative, but rarely neutral. You can defuse or create customer skepticism.

Your presence and ability to relate through your
handshake,
eye contact,
body language,
smile,
posture,

clothing,

voice

and tone

help create that fast but often indelible impression.

Everything in your greeting and introduction instantly speaks for you and can pigeonhole you in your customer's mind. Things like questionable dress or being late can take you out of a positive or neutral zone and quickly send you into a negative one.

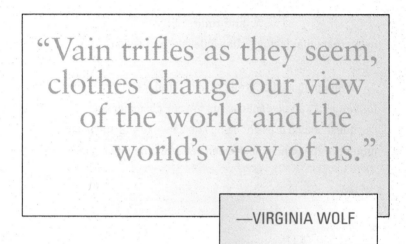

"Vain trifles as they seem, clothes change our view of the world and the world's view of us."

—VIRGINIA WOLF

HIGH-MILEAGE RAPPORT

Of course your customers are busy and so are you. That doesn't mean there isn't time for rapport. You have choices when it comes to rapport based on the relationship and situation. What is the relationship? Are you with a prospect or a customer? What are the rapport cues? What is the customer's approach? What is the organizational culture—more laid-back or formal? And finally, how much time do you have for the call?

In almost all situations, rapport-building during the opening is more than optional. It is expected. **Rapport is a part of human relationships.** While you should take cues from your customers about their receptivity to rapport, your job is to do all you can to build it.

The most important thing about rapport is that it has to feel authentic. It needs to feel genuine to you. If you respect your customers and care about them it's a lot easier to be sincere. This does not mean you have to love every customer but, unless you are as good an actor as Robert De Niro or Meryl Streep, unless you are sincere, your rapport building is likely to come across as fake.

"The rule is,
 if it is designed to
   advance your career,
    it isn't conversation."

—JUDITH MARTIN
Miss Manners

The key is to prepare for rapport and few salespeople do this. To create meaningful rapport, ideally prepare to connect on two levels: personal and business. If you are building both personal and business rapport, always start with personal rapport—the more specific and interesting to the customer, the better.

While you should always be prepared, preparing for rapport doesn't replace spontaneous rapport. Be alert to more compelling immediate rapport cues that are presented in the environment, such as a class photo of the executive development program the customer has proudly displayed on the wall, a collection of model racing cars prominently lining a shelf, or family photos on a desk.

Personal Rapport

A personal rapport topic can either be something you have prepared or something triggered by a cue in the customer's environment. One of the best ways to build rapport is to ask a rapport question or make a statement that invites a response. Here are some examples:

- I read that you are chairing the… event for the Chamber. It looks like a terrific event … How did you get involved?

13

- How are you finding…?

- I saw a photo of your son's team in the paper. How long has he been playing?

- I looked at your Web site. I see you added animation… (assuming this is not the topic of your sales call). It looks great… How did you think of…?

- This collection is great. When did you start collecting?

- So, how was Jane's birthday party?

- I read about the groundbreaking ceremony for Saturday. You must be very proud.

- I've been familiar with your name for a long while. How did you get into the industry?

- How long have you known Bill (referral source)?

Of course, there are many topics for personal rapport including comments on the area, the weather, or other observations or opinions (avoiding sex, politics, and religion!), but almost nothing is more effective than showing interest in the customer by asking rapport questions.

Business Rapport

Business rapport can be anything related to a business topic that is not directly connected to the objective of your call. Topics could be a conference you attended, an article in the press about the customer's recent promotion, or a change in the customer's organization. For example,

I understand you presented... in the... conference. How do you manage to do so much?

Sometimes the lines between personal and business rapport merge depending on how you use a topic. The key is to make sure you don't use a rapport topic that is related to your call objective that will inadvertently move you out of the connecting phase too soon. For example, a referral can be used as a topic for personal or business rapport but it can also be used to help you transition to Step 2, Explore, depending on how you use it. If you say, *I appreciate John's introducing me to you. He mentioned you are looking for... "* you lead into Step 2, Explore, too soon before you have completed the other Step 1 Actions. Many salespeople fall into this trap.

15

Rapport Topics

As for what to talk about, the more customized to the interest of the customer the better. But in truth, rapport isn't so much about the topic as it is about creating a human connection. Almost any topic will work as long as it is genuine and noncontroversial. And don't complain about things like getting the middle seat on the airplane, traffic, or a head cold, because your customer may think you are indirectly blaming the sales call for your woes!

> Rapport building is about
> the customer, not you.

Rapport Spotlight

RULE OF THUMB: The focus of rapport should be on the customer, not you. Talking about yourself is not the best way to build rapport. Of course, it's appropriate to share something about yourself, but then *immediately*

**volley the attention
back to the
customer.**

For example, if your customer tells you he or she lived in Chicago, and you went to school there, you should share that, add something positive about Chicago, but then quickly shift the focus back on the customer by asking a question such as where in Chicago he or she lived or how long, etc. When one salesperson mentioned that she had gone to school in Chicago and then proceeded to tell the executive about her experience at the university after about 15 seconds, the potential customer said, "Well, if you'll excuse me." Had she used a rapport question to bring the focus back on him, the dialogue with this executive may have gone on longer.

Another case in point—when a philanthropist was asked why he decided against making a gift to his alma mater, he blamed the director of development, whom he described as self-focused. "She," he said "spent almost all the entire dinner discussing her upcoming wedding and recent move to the area. In fact out of courtesy I asked her about herself but I felt it was her job to refocus us back to my goals."

Time for Rapport

As for how much time to spend on rapport building, the length of time can vary from situation to situation, culture to culture.

My advice is to allocate a minimum of 5 to 8 percent of the call to Step 1. So in a 40-minute call, *aim* to spend about 5 minutes, with most of that time being spent on rapport. Of course, the time allocated can be much longer or as short as the hello and thank you for meeting, based on the customer, situation, relationship, call objective, time, and culture. As culture studies have shown, on the west coast of the United States, more time is usually spent on rapport building than, for example, in most big U.S. cities on the east coast. Also, entire regions such as Latin America and Asia are known for more extensive rapport building.

Receptivity to Rapport

While you want to do all you can to establish rapport, read the situation to gauge the customer's interest in "chit chat." If the customer signals "no rapport"—with a curt answer, a flat tone, a protective posture, or a direct suggestion to "get to business," take the cue. If customers express no interest in rapport, their reasons can be as innocuous as a tight schedule or as troublesome as a preference not to buy from you.

With customers who rebuff overtures of rapport as the call begins, it is often possible to find opportunities to connect later during the call, toward the end of the call, or, if necessary, in subsequent calls. Fortunately, almost all customers welcome appropriate rapport and are happy to give you a few minutes to connect on a more personal level.

Rapport beyond the Opening

Although rapport building is primarily thought of as something that happens at the start of the call, and while it is mostly concentrated there, rapport can and should be built and maintained throughout the call. For example, in the middle of a discussion of needs you can pick up on a side comment the customer shares such as, *"Actually, I was trained in your field."* By showing interest, your short tangent will help you learn more about the customer and strengthen your personal connection. Then you can get back to the topic at hand.

Rapport can extend beyond words and gestures to actions, whether it is a tennis game with a customer, dinner, or tickets to a show. **Actions speak louder than words.** So demonstrate your interest in the customer to strengthen rapport with things like offering your customer your cell phone number for access to you on a weekend, sending a birthday card, and finding ways to do things you don't get paid for.

19

Transitioning Out of Rapport

Many salespeople become concerned that if they begin rapport they might never get to the business at hand. Often, just the opposite is the issue. Not enough time is spent on real rapport building. Don't be too eager to cut rapport short. Unless you are with a customer who has a pattern of using rapport to avoid getting to the issues or making a commitment, take advantage of rapport time. However, if you feel that rapport is going on too long, moving on is not difficult. Wait for the customer to

take a breath

and begin your move to Action 2 by summarizing how you got there and leveraging your preparation.

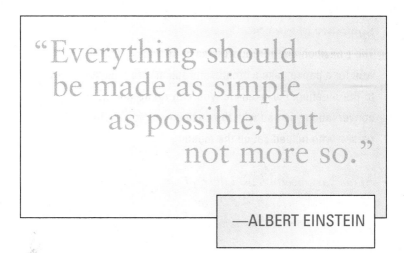

"Everything should
be made as simple
as possible, but
not more so."

—ALBERT EINSTEIN

ACTION 2: Summary of Events and Leverage Preparation

Summary of Events

The transition out of rapport is easy. To avoid shift-shock, simply wait for a pause, take a breath, and summarize the events that led to the meeting. For example, you can recap the last meeting or conversation you had with the customer or you might refer to the person who helped set up the meeting.

At our last meeting, we talked about... and...

or

When we spoke on the phone you mentioned...

or

I very much appreciate Bob's introducing me to you...
He mentioned that you were thinking about... and I
appreciate the chance to meet with you about this.

By referring to how you got there you can comfortably move out of rapport.

Leverage Preparation

Once you've summarized how you got there, immediately describe what you did to prepare. Customers like to know they are on your mind. By showing you have given thought to the meeting, you let your customers know you value their time and are ready to maximize it. It takes just a second to get credit for your preparation. For example:

I've given a lot of thought to...

or

I've visited your Web site (store)... ,
I've tried your product...,

or

I've spoken with my team members about our phone conversation...,
I spoke with your manager of...,

or

I've put together examples of some of the successful projects we completed for... X, Y customers.

or

Since our last meeting I've developed a...

By positioning your preparation you earn points and respect from your customers and you may even earn more time.

Action 2 takes but a few seconds. And once you've done this, prospects at this point are more inclined to be open or at least neutral toward you. Current customers will be reminded why they chose you in the first place.

Then move on to Action 3.

ACTION 3: Dual Purpose and Check

Dual Purpose

To further focus your customer, it is important to state the purpose of your call to clarify why you are there and to make sure you and your customer are on the same page. The call purpose has two dimensions: The first establishes you as customer-focused by making it clear you are there to learn more about the customer's needs. The second clarifies the reason for the meeting with potential benefits to the customer.

For example, *"Today I'd like to learn more about your objectives for... and then share with you our... to see how we may... (customer benefit)."* By stating you are there to learn more about the customer you also help prepare the customer for an interactive dialogue. Stating you are there to learn more also helps prevent you from talking about your products in a generic way before you understand the customer's needs. By then stating your purpose, you clarify why you are there.

Rather than beginning to describe your purpose with a comment such as, *I'm here to discuss our product...* say something like, *I'm here to learn more about your objectives.* The difference is the difference between night and day. Your words tell whether you are product-focused or customer-focused. Use your words to venture on a probing path to **learn more about your customer**.

If you plan to cover multiple topics or if the call has multiple objectives, further clarify your purpose by identifying the key points on your agenda. For example, *Today, I'd like to learn more about your objectives..., you mentioned seeing your facility, and then I'd like to share with you the projects we completed for... then review our... and go over... and results...* or *For today's agenda I thought we might...* (bullet out the key points of your agenda). While you must prepare and clarify your agenda, unless the call is more formal or complex, you need not create a written agenda for distribution.

Check

Once you have clarified your purpose and/or reviewed your agenda, immediately ask for feedback to make sure you are fulfilling your customer's expectations for the call and to identify any other areas that the customer cares about that should be included. For example, you could ask,

How does that meet your expectations?

or

How does that sound?

By asking for feedback you learn how in sync you are with your customer's objectives and you get buy-in, which increases customer receptivity.

In most situations there will be alignment, but if there is a disconnect, it is important to learn about it as soon as possible. When one salesperson identified a topic that she planned to cover, her surprised customer pushed back. By checking she learned that her liaison hadn't been up-to-date on the customer's priorities. Aware her agenda was not on target, the salesperson was able to adjust the agenda quickly and lead a successful meeting. Even when you are sure your agenda is on point, checking the agenda is still worth doing because by asking, versus appearing to presume the customer is in agreement, you give your customer the sense of control and choice that foster buy-in.

27

Credentialize

Sometimes you will find it necessary to credentialize your organization and/or yourself. Credentializing goes a step beyond stating your name, role, and organization. When you credentialize you establish your credentials to help shape how a prospect or new contact in a present relationship views your organization or you. Credentializing usually fits in right after you check your agenda and before you transition out of the opening. Since credentializing is something you are called on to do often, prepare your core message about yourself and your organization. Make it clear, easy to follow, and concise. Be able to deliver it in about one to two minutes at most. Adapt that core message to customize for each customer.

ACTION 4: Transition to Needs

At this point you are ready to conclude your opening. This is a fork in the road. About 60 percent of salespeople consistently take the product path rather than the probing path.

One of the biggest mistakes salespeople make, which can cost them business, begins with a misstep here. Too often salespeople either present immediately or ask too few questions before presenting. The result is the same either way. The presentation almost always is generic and the interest of the customer wanes.

Instead, if you take the probing path, because of everything you have done so far, you can capitalize on your customer's likely willingness to talk about his or her needs. You have "given" and now it is time to "get." You are ready to transition to Step 2.

To transition out of the opening, ask your customer if you may ask a few questions. Preface this request with a customer benefit. For example,

Before I share with you our…, so I can focus on what is most important to you, may I ask a few questions?

or

29

So I may focus on your priorities, I'd like to first learn more about... May I ask a few questions?

or

Before I go over our capabilities (ideas, recommendations...) to understand,... may I ask what...?

When hearing about this step, some salespeople ask how this would work if this were a follow-up meeting and they had already identified needs. This is certainly a valid question. Naturally, there is a buildup of information from one call to another. When you already have a good understanding of needs, it would be inappropriate and annoying to your customers for you to rehash the same information.

Nevertheless, even when you believe you have a full understanding of needs, begin each new call with a few probes to make sure you are up to date on any new developments. Asking some questions equally helps you re-engage your customers and primes them to actively participate in the meeting. Rule of thumb: *Before presenting your capabilities, get customer input.*

If you show you are **prepared** and **interested** to learn about the customer's needs, the number of customers who will refuse to talk about them will be few and far between. If customers push back by saying, I'd like to hear what you have to say, comply but don't go too far out on a product limb alone. Give a minute or two of information and then ask,

How does this sound?

or

How does that match up with what you were thinking?

Most customers are unable to resist giving their view.

Customers who still refuse to share information about their needs could be signaling a lack of interest in the product or negative feelings about their relationship with you or your organization. Or they simply may lack time.

Optional Time Check

Most likely, as you scheduled the sales call, you established how much time you would have for the meeting. Therefore, a time check usually isn't necessary. However, if you want to check if the time frame still works, do so after you have positioned the benefits of meeting and before the transition to needs. For example, *You mentioned in our phone call we'd have about 45 minutes. How does that work for you?* or *Does that still work for you?* But if you have established the time frame for the call in advance, unless the customer has a pattern of cutting meetings short, this isn't necessary.

A HIGH-POWERED OPENING

You may be thinking that the call would be over by the time you do all of this. True, there are 4 Actions in the Connect Step. However, once you master and put the actions to use, you will see that all together they take but a few minutes. The advantage is you are then completely poised to explore needs.

> For example, *Hi Nancy. I'm Carol Marino with X. Thanks for taking the time today to meet. John felt that we should meet* (for first meetings). *He is a great guy and was very complimentary about you. He mentioned you've just moved... How are you finding the area...?* (personal rapport building)... *I read in the paper that the company is opening offices in...*

Have you been involved...? (business rapport)... *As I said, John felt we should meet to... since we have done extensive work in... with... John gave me a little background and in preparing for our meeting I read about your new strategy on your Web site. I've also spoken with our specialists* (summary of events and leverage preparation). *Today I'd like to learn more about your objectives for... and... share with you our... How does that sound?* (dual-purpose and check)... *So I may focus on what is important to you in... before I... may I ask a few questions to get a better understanding of your objectives for...* (transition to needs)?

The main variable in Step 1 is the time spent on rapport. It's easy to know when you begin Step 1. But it is very important to be aware of what makes up Connect so you don't cut it short and you are aware when you are ending it. What happens between the hello and the end of Step 1 establishes your connection, and what happens when you exit Step 1 sets the direction of the dialogue to follow.

33

STEP ONE: CONNECT

☐ **ACTION 1:** Greet/High-Mileage Rapport

☐ **ACTION 2:** Summary of Events/Leverage Preparation

☐ **ACTION 3:** Dual Purpose and Check

☐ **ACTION 4:** Transition to Needs

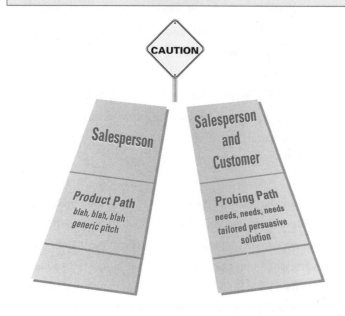

TOOLS AND ACTION PLAN

■ To reinforce Step 1, Connect, use the Connect Pre-Call Planner and Connect Post-Call Debrief on pages 36 to 39 before and after your next few sales calls.

■ To help you prepare, go to your prospect or customer's Web site, use your resources, check your CRM, tap into colleagues, and make a pre-call phone call to help you set your agenda.

■ To download tools to your computer, phone, or handheld, please visit **http://www.richardson.com/ Resource-Center/Perfect-Selling-Tools/** and enter Username: **perfectseller** and Password: **Richardson**).

CONNECT PRE-CALL PLANNER

Customer: _____   *Date:* _____

Call Objective _____

■ **Greet/Introduce**
_____

■ **Rapport**

■ Personal Rapport
_____

_____

■ Business Rapport
_____

■ **Summary of Events/Leverage Preparation**

■ Recap what led to the sales call
_____

_____

■ Leverage your preparation
_____

■ **Dual Purpose and Check**

■ Statement to learn about customer objectives/get update
_____

(To access Perfect Selling tools and test please go to
http://www.richardson.com/Resource-Center/Perfect-Selling-Tools/
and enter Username: **perfectseller** and Password: **Richardson**)

■ Potential benefit to customer

_____

_____

■ Checking question for alignment

_____

_____

■ **Credentialize Self and/or Organization (if needed)**

_____

■ **Transition to Explore**

_____

■ Gain customer's agreement to answer a few questions

_____

_____

(To access Perfect Selling tools and test please go to
http://www.richardson.com/Resource-Center/Perfect-Selling-Tools/
and enter Username: **perfectseller** and Password: **Richardson**)

CONNECT POST-CALL DEBRIEF

Customer: _____   **Date:** _____

Call Objective _____

	Yes	No	Notes/Action Steps
Greet/Introduce ■ Greeted/introduced with strong presence ■ Made good impression in a "blink"	☐	☐	

	Yes	No	Notes/Action Steps
High-Mileage Rapport ■ Built personal rapport ■ Built business rapport	☐	☐	

	Yes	No	Notes/Action Steps
Summary/Leverage Preparation ■ Summarized what led to call and leveraged preparation	☐	☐	

©2008 Linda Richardson

(To access Perfect Selling tools and test please go to
http://www.richardson.com/Resource-Center/Perfect-Selling-Tools/
and enter Username: **perfectseller** and Password: **Richardson**)

	Yes	No	Notes/Action Steps
Dual Purpose/Check	☐	☐	
■ Positioned dual purpose of learning more and focus of call with customer benefits			

	Yes	No	Notes/Action Steps
Transition to Explore	☐	☐	
■ Transitioned by asking for customer's agreement for you to probe			

■ Will you continue to work on Step 1, Connect, or move on to Step 2, Explore?

☐ Continue to work on Step 1

☐ Move to Step 2

(To access Perfect Selling tools and test please go to
http://www.richardson.com/Resource-Center/Perfect-Selling-Tools/
and enter Username: **perfectseller** and Password: **Richardson**)

TWO
2

EXPLORE

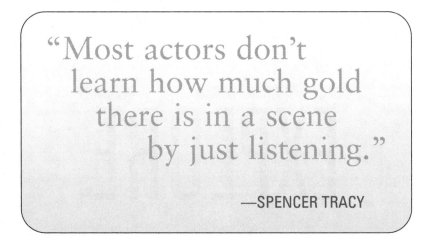

"Most actors don't
learn how much gold
there is in a scene
by just listening."

—SPENCER TRACY

THE BEDROCK

Customer needs are the bedrock of the sales dialogue. Your questions generate energy and your listening allows you to mine the gold that is in every dialogue. The perfect call for customers starts when they feel their needs are understood.

Just as a straight line is the fastest distance between two points, understanding customer needs is the fastest route to making a sale. Nothing much good can happen in a sale without a solid grounding in customer needs. Without questioning and listening it is almost impossible to know what your customer thinks and wants to achieve or for you to turn your products into customer solutions.

It is a poor understanding of needs, more than a weak budget or strong competitors, that poses the greatest obstacle to winning business. To paraphrase Spencer Tracy, "Most salespeople don't realize how much gold there is in a sales call by just listening." By asking questions and listening to your customers, you can internalize the customer's point of view so the customer sees you as an ally versus someone out for a sale.

Do you understand your customers' needs?

Most likely your answer is yes, and you are right — to a point. You ask questions and listen to answers in order to understand what your customers are trying to achieve. But as the expression goes, there is understanding and then there is understanding. Questioning and listening open the way to understanding. If you think about your sales calls, what is your talk/listen ratio? At a minimum, your listening should be equal to your talking. In fact, if you think of the 5 Steps as bands, Step 2, Explore, would be the broadest band.

Unfortunately, while understanding customer needs is recognized as critical to selling, Step 2 often gets short-shrift. Traditionally, salespeople have thought of themselves in the role of the "answer man," therefore, it is easy for them to fall into a mode of telling, not questioning and listening. Salespeople are also action-oriented and listening can seem too time-consuming and passive. Additionally, there is the concern among salespeople that if they ask questions they could lose control of the dialogue or find themselves in areas they are not prepared to discuss or don't want to pursue.

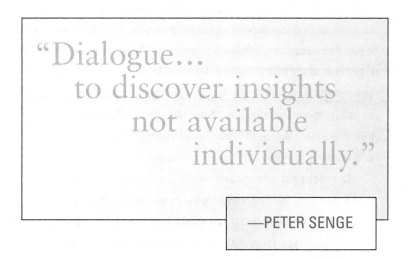

"Dialogue...
to discover insights
not available
individually."

—PETER SENGE

Perhaps the hardest part of questioning is developing the discipline to continue to ask questions. It takes patience to listen and awareness to resist the instinct to jump in with an answer or view. If you can suspend judgment and probe as if you were an **investigative detective** before leaping to solutions, you could change the entire dynamic of your dialogue. It is when you are questioning and listening in "detective mode" that you create a true dialogue. "Dialogue" from Greek *dialogos* means to learn — and learning is more about gaining, not giving, information.

Questions not only unearth needs, but they also help you direct your customer's thinking. They get the customer to focus on the topics you want on the table. If you simply introduce a topic from your perspective you can provoke defensiveness from your customer. Just charging ahead and giving your view before you know the customer's perspective is likely to cause oppositional thinking on your customer's part. However, by using questions to broach a topic, in a sense you are using the "back door," and with the customer you jointly get the topic on the table.

The quality of your questions shows your customer that you can add value. Your questions help customers think through their needs more fully. And your questions help you maintain rapport by demonstrating your interest in the customer. Most important-ly, questions let you listen and learn what it takes to meet the customer's needs.

As you think about how you use questions, be honest.

What questions do you ask?
Do you feel you ask enough questions?

Understanding customer needs would be a lot easier if you could ask just one question: What are your needs? This may seem like a perfectly reasonable way to find out about needs, but in most situations this question is too broad. Customer answers are likely to be equally broad, leaving you with general or evasive replies. This question also puts the onus on the customer and makes the customer responsible to do too much of the work. Moreover, it assumes the customer has already thought about all of the needs your product or service could fulfill.

Based on my extensive work with salespeople, salespeople run into trouble with their questioning in one or more of these ways:

- **Presenting too early:** Describing features and benefits before probing for needs.
- **Asking too few questions:** Missing critical questions.
- **Using limited kinds of questions:** Focusing solely on technical vs. starting with strategic questions.
- **Asking questions without a logical flow:** Questioning in a disorganized and incomplete way and starting with technical questions.
- **Skimming the surface:** Moving on to the next question on their "list" instead of drilling down to explore the customer's answer to hit "pay dirt."
- **Asking too late:** Showing interest in customer's needs late in the sales cycle — only after the customer has lost interest in the sale.

Questions are to selling what fuel is to an engine.

Questioning is much more than a skill. It is a mindset. How you think about and use questions during a sales call reveals a lot about how you see your customers. By asking questions, you signal to your customers that you feel they are smart and perceptive. You show you believe they know their business and have the capacity to tell you how to sell to them. How you use questioning broadcasts how you see yourself—expert, consultant, authority, collaborator, teacher, coach, partner…

Good questioning requires a discipline that is second-nature. Salespeople who are good at asking questions understand deep down they can add the most value and be most persuasive by using questions. Strong probers are strong across the board when it comes to questioning because for them probing is a way of thinking, a natural instinct. They know how to probe without sounding like a district attorney.

49

The discipline of probing is well worth developing. For example, one salesperson who sold flooring to schools realized to achieve his quarterly objectives he would have to uptier to the superintendent of schools. But his hard-earned meeting with the superintendent failed to help him achieve his objective. After building rapport he showed a slide presentation of his capabilities. At the end of this, the superintendent said, "I found a few slides interesting but all the ones on carpeting don't apply to us since we don't use carpeting." The mindset that led this salesperson to show the slide presentation before probing was the same mindset that caused him to miss the chance to probe what slides were of interest to the superintendent. Had the salesperson had the discipline of probing, the meeting could have had a different ending.

Having a structure for your questions is a way to create the discipline. The Explore Step is built on 4 Actions. These actions provide a flow so your questioning is organized and builds on itself. You can leverage your knowledge and experience as you phrase your questions and maximize your customer's answers.

THE 4 ACTIONS ARE:

☐ **ACTION 1: Objectives Questions:**

*What are your **objectives** for ...?*

> drill down

☐ **ACTION 2: Current Situation Questions:**

*What are you **currently** doing in ...?*

> drill down

☐ **ACTION 3: Technical Questions:**

***How many** ...? (product related details)*

> drill down

☐ **ACTION 4: Future and Personal Needs Questions:**

*What are **future needs** you anticipate?*

> drill down

*What is **most important** to you?*

> drill down

Customers must feel they've been heard.

The sequence of the questions in each Action step moves from broader, strategic questions to more narrow technical questions. If the idea of a fixed sequence sounds mechanical, so be it. After all, there is a mechanical (step-by-step) element to everything creative from Nascar racing to ballet. The art lies in the execution. Asking questions, listening, and then drilling down help you position yourself with your customers as a trusted advisor—the one they call first when they have a need.

Not a "List" of Questions

The 4 Actions would indeed be mechanical if they were only a list of consecutive questions. Instead each question triggers **drill-down questions based on the customer's response**. Your job is to listen so that you can probe the customer's answer versus move to your next question or start to tell. Having a sequence to your questioning will help you gain critical information. Digging deeper into your customers' answers will give you a competitive edge because you will have a deeper understanding of the customer's needs. Each question you ask opens a door to a drill-down question until you gain the level of information you need—before going on to the next action.

While the 4 Actions guide you in your line of questioning, the actual content, tone, and wording of the questions you ask are yours—natural to you, reflecting your knowledge, and completely customized to the situation because the drill-down questions you ask are based on your customer's answers.

Let's look inside each Action.

ACTION 1: Objectives Questions— the Best *First* Question

This first question you ask is a pivotal moment in the call. You have worked so hard to lead up to this question. You have connected with rapport. You have leveraged your preparation. You have positioned your purpose and benefits. You have asked for and gotten the customer's agreement to answer a few questions. You have earned the right to ask questions. You have "given" so you can now "get." You are poised to ask this "magical" first question.

Ask the Objectives Question

This question is magical because it gives you a "flying carpet" view you would not otherwise see. By asking, "What are your objectives for …?" you show you are more of a strategic thinker and you gain insight beyond data.

How you position this question makes a difference in the kind of answer you get. Lead into this broad question with a benefit to the customer, a reason for asking, or state what you know about the situation to encourage your customer to give a more complete answer.

For example, if your purpose is to discuss how you might support the customer in international expansion you can ask,

"In regard to your international expansion, to see how we might support you, what are your objectives for …?"

or

"I read about your… so I can focus on what would be most relevant to you … What are your objectives for…?"

or

"In your phone call you mentioned your priority is to … What are your objectives for …?"

The objective question, as straightforward as it is, is challenging for even experienced salespeople to ask. In a coaching session it can take several tries for them to ask, "What are your objectives for…?"

Once you ask the objective question, treat the customer's answer as sacred. Don't say or do anything to stop the flow of what the customer shares. I cringe when salespeople break the magic spell of the Objective Question by interrupting with an unrelated question or by beginning to present information. They miss a chance to learn and connect.

As your customer describes his or her objective, you must scan the customer's answers for broad words. As you mentally scan, look for words that are vague, ambiguous, emotionally charged, or underscored. Acknowledge these and ask drill-down questions to learn more. Spend time asking about and continuing to probe customers' objectives.

Dialogue is how you get ideas from and to customers.

You almost can't spend too much time on the objectives questions. This is the time to probe further to explore your customer's response and use it as a platform for drilling down. For example, if the customer says, "We want to expand into new global markets and get our people on the ground," first acknowledge this goal. Then probe to learn about the "global business." Listen and continue to acknowledge and probe further to understand more about the new markets and why there is a need for people on the ground. Or if your customer says, "One of our critical objectives is to become one of the top five… by the year…" acknowledge and probe the reason driving the objective, why the target date, and so on. If the customer says, "We are looking for a partner to make the acquisition," probe what the customer means by partner, if the customer has any companies as a partner in mind, why the partner strategy, and if the customer has an acquisition candidate in mind. If you gloss over the answer to an objectives question, you will miss critical information.

A rule of thumb for need dialogue is to acknowledge and probe your customer's objectives answers at least once before going on to the next question. Because you will be probing more, acknowledgment of what the customer says is very important to keep the customer motivated to provide answers.

Once you understand the objective your customer has described, and you've probed it, check if there are any other objectives and probe those. For example, *"I understand… is important, especially with… I appreciate your taking the time to help me fully understand this. What other objectives do you have?"* Not until your customer tells you there are no other objectives, should you shift gears and go on to Action 2. If your customer identifies several objectives at one time, probe to learn as much as you can about each objective before trying to learn the priority of these needs.

Many salespeople aren't sure what their first question will be. Often for their first question they ask a technical question such as, "What are you doing now in...?" "How many... do you use each month?" While these are great questions, they are not the best first question because they are narrow. While asking almost any question is better than immediately presenting information without probing, technical questions are too tactical to begin a deeper needs dialogue. Start with the objectives questions.

ACTION 2: Current Situation Question

Once you understand the big picture it is time to get details.

Ask, "What are you currently doing in…?" or "How do you currently…?"

and continue to scan your customer's answers so you can acknowledge and drill down deeper. Probe to understand the level of satisfaction. For example, if you ask about the current situation and your customer says, "We tried several things but were not happy with the results. It's been very frustrating. Actually, that is why we are talking to a few companies," you could say,

"I'm sure that is disappointing (empathy/ acknowledgment). We're happy to speak with you about this since it's an area in which we've had significant success. To help me think about how we could help, what things have you tried?"

Then probe—drill down—to discover how that has worked and what the customer wants to change. And since the customer introduced the topic of competitors this also is a great opportunity to ask, "You mentioned talking to other companies. To understand what you are considering, who are you talking with?"

Word by word
customers get it.
Word by word
you get it.

ACTION 3: Technical Questions

Once you understand the customer's current situation, a natural extension of this dialogue is for you to ask your key technical/product-related questions such as, "How many... do you have? What kind of... are you using? How are the... structured?" so that you have all the data you need to understand the situation, priorities, and preferences to maximize the capabilities you will propose.

> If you want your customers to be excited about your solutions, you have to be passionate about their needs.

ACTION 4: Future and Personal Needs Questions

Future Needs

By now, you might think you are ready to start talking about your products or ideas. But if you continue to probe just a little more you can gain two benefits. First, you can show you are relationship- versus transaction-oriented. Second, you will learn information that will help you fine-tune and differentiate your solution by building in what is on the horizon.

For example, you can ask: "So that I can take into consideration any future initiatives that could influence what we recommend, what should we be aware of that may be coming up?"

True to form, continue to acknowledge and probe as necessary. Probing beyond the immediate need takes discipline, but the payoff is more than worth the few minutes this takes.

Personal Needs

Then probe personal needs to further connect and gain additional insights. Customers buy from salespeople they believe understand what they want and care about what is at stake for them. Is the customer primarily motivated by a desire to dominate market share? Is the customer motivated more by being recognized as a tough negotiator? Is it important for the customer to institute a change? Is the customer's job on the line? Don't assume you know what is personally motivating your customer and charge ahead. Customers make decisions based on how a solution meets not only their business needs but also what is driving them personally.

Getting personal insights takes tact, sensitivity, and the ability to seize opportunities your customers give you to probe. Do not directly or aggressively ask about personal drivers in most situations.

Customers let you know in words, tone, and with body language what personally motivates them. Customers provide cues such as word emphasis or a pointed delivery of a phrase, which if you pick up you can probe. For example, a customer might say, "I have a lot riding on this" (underscoring 'a lot'). By showing empathy and interest by asking, "I know this is very important to you.

63

When you say 'a lot riding on this,' in what way?", you will learn about the customer's personal drivers and strengthen your personal connection.

Even if your customer doesn't provide openings for you to probe personal motivators, you can proactively ask questions. For example,

"I know how much focus there is on this initiative. What is the thing that is most important to you?"

How you phrase these questions must be respectful and sometimes indirect. Avoid the question, "What keeps you up at night?" as it can make a customer feel defensive. Aside from being overused by some salespeople, this question can be too personal and also rather presumptuous. Maybe the customer sleeps just fine!

To summarize, good salespeople know how to gain insights. Your job is to listen attentively, acknowledge what the customer says, and continue to probe until you know enough to offer a winning solution.

To understand more than surface needs you have to dig deeper.

IMPLEMENTATION QUESTIONS

As you ask questions about objectives, current situation, and so on, you will likely get information about implementation. Implementation information includes data on the customer's decision process, time frames, budget, competitors the customer is considering, how the customer feels about them, and how the customer feels you compare, as well as compelling events driving the purchase decision. For example, as a part of describing his or her objectives a customer may include the time frame or the compelling event driving the objective—such as, "We are trying to... and we need the system in by the second quarter because..."

However, when any implementation information has not been discussed in the course of the dialogue, it is critical for you to ask questions proactively. For example,

- **Decision process:** "Once you review this, who else will be involved in your decision process?"
- **Competitors:** "So I understand your thinking and the kind of things you are considering, who else are you talking to?"
- **Time frame:** "So we can meet your expectations, what are your time frames?" or "You mentioned X date was firm. So I fully understand this, may I ask why this date is firm?"
- **Budget:** "So I can have a sense of what you are thinking as I put my proposal together, what is the budget you have set?"

> Your questions give you
> a clear window into the
> mind of your customer.

EXPLORING IN FOLLOW-UP CALLS

If you are selling a useful product or service, chances are your customers already know something about it, and throughout the sales cycle will keep learning. Therefore, you must continue to learn what your customers know, how they think, and what it will take to sell to them. Unless you continue to probe throughout the sales cycle you may face unwelcome surprises.

Certainly in follow-up sales calls with your customer, as mentioned earlier, it isn't necessary to go over ground already covered. But because customer needs and knowledge evolve, it is necessary to continue to probe and listen to stay abreast of new developments. During the sales cycle customers continue to learn more about their needs and what options are available to them. They can search the Web and/or talk with your competitors. Probing and listening in each contact will keep you up to date, reinforce your customer focus, and keep your customers engaged.

In follow-up calls, use questions to:

refine your understanding of needs
gain new information
get feedback
know where to put emphasis
learn about changes
understand new priorities
identify and get input
from new influencers
or decision makers.

CONSTRUCTING, PREFACING, DRILLING DOWN

Since it is likely you will be doing more probing than may have been your practice, it is important to support your questioning strategy with effective skills that will make both the customer and you comfortable with the probing.

There are three probing skills individually or combined that take questioning to the level of "art" and create robust dialogues.

The skills are:

- **Constructing**
- **Prefacing**
- **Drilling down**

Constructing

Questions are constructed as open-ended or closed-ended. Almost all salespeople know the value of structuring their questions so the questions are open- versus closed-ended. Open-ended questions are what- and why-type questions that allow you to explore topics and encourage a robust dialogue. Closed-ended questions lead to limited yes-no answers. Ask closed-ended questions when you seek a definitive answer, such as asking for your action step. But remember, open-ended questions lead to rich dialogues.

Prefacing

Prefacing is a powerful skill in which you prepare the customer for a question and encourage him or her to give a more complete response. You can preface a question by introducing it with a benefit to the customer, acknowledging or empathizing with something the customer has said or you know to be relevant to the customer, by exchanging information and leveraging your knowledge, or by positioning a strength of your organization or product, a "minicommercial."

For example:

Prefacing with Benefits to the Customer:

> *So I have a better sense of how we could*
> *support you in this, what are...?*

Prefacing with Acknowledgment:

> *You mentioned you have tried a few initiatives.*
> *What kind of things have you tried?*

Prefacing by Trading Information/Leveraging Your Knowledge:

> *We are seeing an increase in...*
> *with some of our...*
> *customers who are seeking to...*
> *What is leading you in that direction?*

Prefacing with a "Minicommercial":

> *You mentioned your interest in X company.*
> *We have had a strong relationship with them*
> *for five years. What is your interest in them?*

By providing a benefit to your customer (not a benefit to you) you show you've listened and want to understand more to add value. When you use acknowledgment you also show you have listened and also that you respect and care about (not necessarily agree with) what the customer has said. Trading information enables you to leverage your knowledge and experience and fosters reciprocation from the customer. Briefly positioning a strength helps you build your credibility and encourage a response.

Drilling Down

Drill-down is the skill of deep dialogue. It allows you to gain the fullest understanding of the customer's needs and thoughts. Acute listening is the key to drilling down. Drilling down requires discipline as you hold back your ideas or your next question. It is also **fueled by a real curiosity to learn more.** Drilling down can require asking several questions. For example, if a customer says she has tried several options, once you acknowledge and probe what those options are, you could probe further to explore the specific options so that you can persuasively shape what you recommend.

Drill-down prevents you from changing topics too soon or from giving your view before you know enough to position a response that will be persuasive and help you win. One salesperson missed an important drill-down question he needed in developing his solution. When his customer asked if his product was generic or customized, he effectively positioned his firm's flexibility in offering both. Unfortunately, he didn't ask which the customer preferred. It seems like such an obvious question. But misses like this happen all the time. By developing a discipline of listening and drilling down you can avoid these common misses.

Drill-down is needed because customers often are not specific. There are so many interpretations and possibilities in what they say. Without drill-down questions you can't know precisely how your customers are thinking. If your customers are vague all you can do is make assumptions about what they mean. Even cooperative customers may not actually answer your question, and unless you drill down you won't get the information you need. For example, when one salesperson asked his customer, "What are your objectives for …?" she replied, "We want to be world class." Remembering the skill of drill-down, instead of moving on to his next question, he mentally backed up and probed "world-class."

Because today's customer knows more, you need to ask more—and talk less.

QUESTIONING TONE

The way you ask questions impacts the answers you get. By using prefacing you can help your customers and you feel comfortable with your questions. A tone that is genuine, that shows interest and curiosity versus being judgmental or self-serving fosters open dialogue. For example, if your customer tells you he or she did X and you think this was not the best approach, try a question like, "John, so I can understand how you plan to use that, may I ask what your thinking was in choosing X?" This will give you the information you need and help you maintain rapport. By contrast, a question such as, "Why would you do that?" stated with a judgmental tone would close down communications.

Are you mostly on
"send" or "receive"?

LEVERAGING WHAT YOU LEARN

By having a progression to how you ask questions, your questioning will be more complete and organized. It will be easier for you
and on your customer. It will help you avoid debilitating pauses in
the dialogue. While a few seconds of silence can be very, very
good, sometimes salespeople stop probing because they are at a
loss as to what questions to ask next—so they start to present or
cut the meeting short.

Questioning and listening are half the battle. The other half is
not wasting the information you gather as you form and describe
your solution. Good note taking will help you maximize the information you gain. Notes are valuable during the call, after the call
to prepare for future calls, and for flawless follow-up.

By having a discipline for how and when you use questions
you can change the nature of the dialogues you have with your
customers. You will learn more and you will give your customers
more talk time. When you do talk, your customers will be more

prepared and willing to listen to you, and what you say will be more persuasive.

As one customer put it, "I can tell if salespeople are interested in me by the questions they ask."

The more time you spend questioning and listening, the less time you will spend *trying* to close.

Change your talk/listen ratio.

STEP TWO: EXPLORE

☐ **ACTION 1: Objectives Questions**

☐ **ACTION 2: Current Situation Questions**

☐ **ACTION 3: Technical Questions**

☐ **ACTION 4: Future Needs and Personal Needs**

EXPLORE PRE-CALL PLANNER

Customer: _____ *Date:* _____

Call Objective _____

- ■ **Objective Questions**
  _____
  _____
  _____

- ■ **Current Situation Questions**
  _____
  _____

- ■ **Technical Questions**
  _____
  _____

- ■ **Future and Personal Needs Questions**
  _____
  _____
  _____
  _____

(To access Perfect Selling tools and test please go to
http://www.richardson.com/Resource-Center/Perfect-Selling-Tools/
and enter Username: **perfectseller** and Password: **Richardson**)

EXPLORE POST-CALL DEBRIEF

Customer: _____ **Date:** _____

Call Objective _____

	Yes	No	Notes/Action Steps
Objectives Questions	☐	☐	
■ Asked objectives question ■ Acknowledged and drilled down ■ Identified other objectives			

	Yes	No	Notes/Action Steps
Current Situation Questions	☐	☐	
■ Probed current situation ■ Acknowledged and drilled down			

	Yes	No	Notes/Action Steps
Technical Questions	☐	☐	
■ Asked objectives question ■ Acknowledged and drilled down			

(To access Perfect Selling tools and test please go to
http://www.richardson.com/Resource-Center/Perfect-Selling-Tools/
and enter Username: **perfectseller** and Password: **Richardson**)

	Yes	No	Notes/Action Steps
Future and Personal Needs Questions	☐	☐	
■ Identified future needs			
■ Acknowledged and drilled down			
■ Identified personal drivers			

■ Will you continue to work on Step 2, Explore, or move on to Step 3, Leverage?

☐ Continue to work on Step 2

☐ Move to Step 3

©2008 Linda Richardson

(To access Perfect Selling tools and test please go to
http://www.richardson.com/Resource-Center/Perfect-Selling-Tools/
and enter Username: **perfectseller** and Password: **Richardson**)

78

The Bedrock of the Sales Call

Questions:

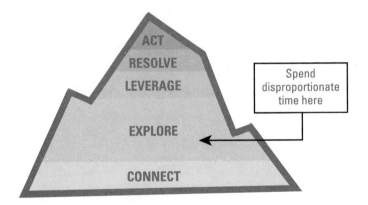

THREE

LEVERAGE

Your words
have the power
to turn products
into solutions.

PRODUCT TO SOLUTION

By listening to your customers, you prepare them to listen to you. With a solid understanding of needs, you are at the next turning point in the perfect sales call: your time to leverage your capabilities by showing how you will satisfy the customer's needs. This is the time when you get to talk about the value you bring. Leverage is the step in the sales call in which you do most, but not all, of the talking—the key is to use your customer's language.

Aside from the word *consultative*, almost no other word in sales has been so misused as the word *solutions*. Most of the time what is called a "solution" boils down to a standard product pitch. Of course it is the fit of your product's features and benefits with the customer's needs that provides the foundation for the solution, but it is the language you use to position your product that turns it into a solution and assures your customers you have heard them and are the one to meet their needs.

83

> Converting products
> to solutions
> isn't conversation—
> it's translation.

We all know companies sell products, but customers buy solutions. Your features and benefits provide the facts that customers need to make decisions. But customers need more than facts to make a commitment. We also know the best technical solution, even at a competitive price, does not always win. This is because buying decisions are in part emotional. Most customers must not only think it is the right decision, they must **feel** it is the right decision. Your role is to help sell to the gut as well as the mind. Beyond your technical solution, it is the connection you make with customers' needs that enables them to buy from you. It is not enough just to understand needs. It is essential to incorporate customer's needs and language into your recommendation to transform your products into solutions.

Salespeople fully leverage their capabilities all too rarely. After working so hard at understanding customer needs, too many salespeople describe their products as if that dialogue hadn't taken place. Instead of incorporating the customer's needs and language, they talk about their products with the language they walked in with. Converting products to solutions isn't small talk. It isn't conversation. It is translation. Once you understand how your product fits the customer's needs, it is your job to reflect that in the solution.

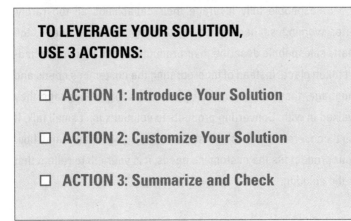

**TO LEVERAGE YOUR SOLUTION,
USE 3 ACTIONS:**

☐ **ACTION 1**: Introduce Your Solution

☐ **ACTION 2**: Customize Your Solution

☐ **ACTION 3**: Summarize and Check

ACTION 1: Introduce Your Solution

Having a structure in and of itself is persuasive. Therefore, start to talk about your solution by introducing it with a structured overview before going into detail. Create the structure by concisely including the headlines of all of the key parts of your solution that support the customer's needs you have identified.

By concisely including all the key elements, you help prepare your customers to listen and you let them know your solution takes all of their needs into account. Moreover, it lets you organize the information that you will be positioning next and makes it easier for your customers to follow and comprehend. By acknowledging needs, you reinforce that you have listened, and by including all parts of the solution, you show that it is complete.

For example, if there are two parts to your solution, you could say, "I understand how important X and Y are and especially to complete them in your time frame. Based on our experience there are two things we recommend to... (customer objective) First, we'd... to... (benefit) and at the same time implement a... and then we would... So that your... (tie to customer need)."

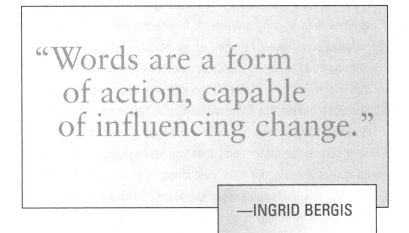

"Words are a form
of action, capable
of influencing change."

—INGRID BERGIS

Simply identify the headlines of what you will cover next. Prioritize them to align with the customer's needs. Most salespeople do the opposite. They directly launch into describing their solution without giving an overview of what they are going to present. Without previewing what will follow, they don't give customers a sense of what is coming or how complete or relevant it is to them. Don't ask for feedback yet since you will not have given sufficient information for the customer to answer intelligently.

Rather than beginning by talking about your products with the words "We offer…" or "Our product…", it is much more persuasive to lead with "We have talked about your needs for X and Y." Start with and incorporate customer needs into every sentence. Generously use the word "you."

By structuring and prioritizing what you say you make it clear to your customers that you have listened and that you *get it* and you *get them*. Better yet, you help your customer *get it*.

Look at the difference:

Generic: "Our support center is located at corporate headquarters with a dedicated account representative there to resolve all customer service issues. Each customer is assigned its own representative. Our account representatives have access to telephone, fax, or e-mail and can leverage our full corporate resources 24/7. And we offer a small back-up team." This is generic—us, us, us!

Customized: "I know how important it is for you to *quickly* and *effectively resolve all customer issues* especially... and avoid that kind of delay by knowing someone is accountable and *dedicated* to you 24/7 (need). There are three things we can do to ensure... First, a fully dedicated account representative whom I work with closely is assigned to you who is there to... for you (benefit) via telephone, fax, or e-mail. Next, you'll also have a small back-up team available for... And, finally, you will have full access to our full corporate resources which give you the... you require for your..."

The last example is customized—the operative word is **you**, the customer. Now you are ready to provide more specifics.

Once you lay out the key parts of the solution you are ready to go directly into the specifics of the solution.

ACTION 2: Customize Your Solution

Immediately after introducing your solution, it is time to substantiate what you have previewed. Start with the priority need and provide customized features and benefits to back it up. Generic features and benefits are factual and neutral. Customized are promotional and persuasive. Tailored solutions show your customers that you have heard them. You need a solid grasp of customers' needs, priorities, and language to customize your products or services. You can increase your persuasiveness if, as a part of presenting your solution or ideas, you provide a relevant example that helps the customer "see" the solution in action.

Thinking "You"

Your customers are bombarded with sales pitches. Your challenge is to make sure when you present your recommendations or ideas that you address what is relevant and important to your customers. Being able to **customize your offerings** is something that has to be worked up to. Once you have prepared, asked questions, and listened, the task remains to use that knowledge to tailor what you say.

91

The features and benefits of your offerings are usually fairly well set. But how you talk about them, what you emphasize, and the language you use is up to you—the more customized, the more persuasive.

A formula for persuasion is:

PRODUCT KNOWLEDGE	CUSTOMER KNOWLEDGE	VALUE ADD	PERSUASIVE SOLUTION
Features	Objectives	Knowledge/ Research	
Benefits	Needs	Experience	
Alternatives	Decision criteria	Resources/ Network	Decision
Value	Desired outcomes	Relationship	to
Examples	Language	Process	Buy
Success stories	Quantifiable value	Strategy and skills	

You leverage your offering by incorporating customer needs into your solutions. Customers want to hear about themselves—

what's important to them and how they can achieve their goals. The best way to leverage your capabilities is to use your product knowledge and value-add in the context of customer needs, and to use their language.

Of all the Steps in the sales call, Leveraging is the most strategic because it requires analyzing your capabilities relative to customer needs and the needs of your organization to determine how to persuasively shape your recommendation to win the business.

Along with Explore, in which you identify needs, Leverage forms the core of the sales call. Connect serves to prepare for this dialogue. Resolve is there to remove road blocks. Act serves to move it forward.

As for how much to say about your capabilities, be concise. It is the Goldilocks theory—not too little, not too much, just right. Think of it as need-to-know versus nice-to-know. Your goal when you position is to create a positive emotional charge. But this takes more than generic product features and benefits. You must show how the products that were designed in your office are solutions that customers want in theirs.

Speak your customer's language.

ACTION 3: Summarize and Check

Summarize

Especially if your solution has multiple parts, use a summary to recap the highlights of what you have described. Begin with the words "In summary," or "So to summarize, we understand... are important to you and we are confident our... will meet your needs." Your summary should be concise and customized to reflect the dialogue you and your customer have been engaged in. This is not the place to introduce anything new. If your solution is simple, you may not have to use a summary. You can simply go on to the final check.

Final Check

Customer feedback is almost always there for the asking. So ask for feedback on what you have presented—especially after you have presented your solution or recommendation. Hopefully, based on all you have done, you will have primed the customer to give positive feedback. But once you have presented your solution and before you ask for a commitment, you must make sure you know how the customer feels about what you've recommended or said. After you have made your recommendation, this *isn't* the time to ask, "What are your thoughts?" or "What questions do you have?" Don't ask for the business—yet! Ask a specific, open-ended question that probes how what you have just presented meets the customer's needs. For example,

"How does... (solution) meet your needs to...?"

... then be silent.

This question isn't always easy to ask. It comes with an element of risk—a possible negative response from your customer. But there is a much greater risk in not knowing exactly how the customer feels about what you have positioned.

It's important to phrase your final checking question very specifically. If you ask a more general question, such as, "How does it sound?" or "What are your thoughts on this?" (which, at other times throughout the dialogue, are essential checking questions), you are likely to get noncommittal answers such as, "I'll think about it" or "I'll get back to you" or "It sounds interesting." Making your recommendation or positioning your solution is a pivotal point and demands a final checking question. Specially ask, "How do you feel about X...? How does it... meet your needs to...?" Because of the directness of this question, you are much more likely to prompt a more definitive response so that you know where you stand and can prepare to close.

Why ask this final checking question before you ask for the business or next action step? It isn't a matter of not being overly aggressive. It is a matter of being smart. The feedback you get will help you gauge how your customer is feeling and thinking and gives you the knowledge and confidence to close or, if you uncover an obstacle, work through it before trying to close.

You have to "get it" before
your customers can "get it."

ALWAYS BE PERSUASIVE

Certainly, it is important to be persuasive when you discuss ideas or position solutions. But you also want to be as persuasive as possible in all phases and aspects of your business dialogues, whether with customers or colleagues, whether you are answering questions, resolving objections, describing your capabilities, or giving background on yourself or your organization. You can become more persuasive by:

maintaining your presence
leveraging your preparation and contacts
remembering to acknowledge or empathize
probing/drilling-down before
giving your perspective
customizing your response to listener needs
using examples or success stories to make things real
checking for feedback

There is an underlying pattern of acknowledging and probing, customizing to customer needs, and asking for feedback that is a part of every Step of the perfect sales call, Step 1 through Step 5. The goal is to make this pattern of communicating the way you do business whether in a sales call, sales letter, e-mail, proposal, or internal team meetings.

Show your customers you get it—
and that you get them.

STEP THREE: LEVERAGE

☐ **ACTION 1:** Structure/Introduce

☐ **ACTION 2:** Customize Your Solution

☐ **ACTION 3:** Summarize/Check for Feedback

LEVERAGE PRE-CALL PLANNER

Customer: _____ *Date:* _____

Call Objective _____

- **Introduce with Structure**

  - Preface with customer needs

    _____

  - Provide overview of all key parts of the
    solution/prioritize to customer needs

    _____

- **Customize Your Solution**

  - Position your customized solution

    _____

    _____

  - Order by priority

    _____

    _____

  - Customize/Use customer's language/
    how organization sees itself

    _____

    _____

  - Keep concise

    _____

    _____

©2008 Linda Richardson

(To access Perfect Selling tools and test please go to
http://www.richardson.com/Resource-Center/Perfect-Selling-Tools/
and enter Username: **perfectseller** and Password: **Richardson**)

■ **Summarize and Check**

■ Customized summary

■ Checking question

©2008 Linda Richardson

(To access Perfect Selling tools and test please go to
http://www.richardson.com/Resource-Center/Perfect-Selling-Tools/
and enter Username: **perfectseller** and Password: **Richardson**)

LEVERAGE POST-CALL DEBRIEF

Customer: _____   *Date:* _____

Call Objective _____

	Yes	No	Notes/Action Steps
Greet/Introduce	☐	☐	
■ Did I tie my solution to my customer's needs?			
■ Did I introduce all key elements of the solution linked to needs before going into detail?			
■ Did I begin with the customer's priority need?			

	Yes	No	Notes/Action Steps
Customize Your Solution	☐	☐	
■ Did I address key needs?			
■ Did I integrate needs?			
■ Was my solution substantive but concise?			

©2008 Linda Richardson

(To access Perfect Selling tools and test please go to
http://www.richardson.com/Resource-Center/Perfect-Selling-Tools/
and enter Username: **perfectseller** and Password: **Richardson**)

	Yes	No	Notes/Action Steps
Summarize and Check	☐	☐	
■ Did I summarize concisely, customized to needs?			
■ Did I check for feedback to understand how the solution addressed the customer's needs?			
■ Was I persuasive?			

■ Will you continue to work on Step 3, Leverage, or move on to Step 4, Resolve?

☐ Continue to work on Step 3

☐ Move to Step 4

(To access Perfect Selling tools and test please go to
http://www.richardson.com/Resource-Center/Perfect-Selling-Tools/
and enter Username: **perfectseller** and Password: **Richardson**)

FOUR

RESOLVE

OPPORTUNITY IN OBJECTIONS

Most salespeople view objections as road blocks—challenges to deal with right up there with closing. Objections stall sales. Objections can even stop sales. But objections can also help you make sales. You are undoubtedly familiar with the frustrations of the stall-and-stop effects of objections on your sales results, but you may not be taking full advantage of the benefits. Rather than being road blocks, in fact, objections can be the road to closing sales, if you can resolve them.

Customer objections present the perfect opportunity for you to take a big step in moving the sale forward. They connect you to the real thinking of your customers. Customers know even customer-focused salespeople have an agenda and, therefore, it is natural for them to treat what salespeople say with a certain level of skepticism. But when your customer objects, since it is the customer who has raised the topic and there is an element of spontaneity to your answer, what you say can be viewed less as a "sales pitch" and more as a sign of your depth. When your answer hits the mark, it not only removes the obstacle, it also strengthens your credibility.

Objections in sales calls are a fact of life. Whether customers mistrust you, want to exert power over you, or really want to learn more from you, customers will always object. Although we are treating **Resolve** as Step 4 in the sales process, customer resistance is the wild card in a sale because it can occur anywhere from hello to thanks and good-by. Ideally, most objections are raised midway through the sales call, which gives you ample time to resolve them, after you have identified needs and presented your solution or ideas and asked for feedback. By asking for feedback you can get objections or questions on the table and work to resolve them.

<blockquote>
Customer objections are
the wild card in the sale.
</blockquote>

It would be great if all it took to resolve objections was the "right" technical response. But when customers object, there is a human dynamic going on. Therefore, it is not just the content of your answer but how you position and deliver that answer that persuades customers. Your technical knowledge is, without a doubt, an essential part of resolving objections. Technical expertise supplies the substance and credibility of your response. Your ability to communicate that expertise, however, supplies the persuasiveness. Whether you carry technical knowledge and experience in your head or rely on a specialist and support materials, how that technical message is communicated determines how persuasive it is.

It might seem the technical knowledge you use to resolve any particular objection would be set in stone. However, because most customer objections are vague the answer to any given objection isn't so clear-cut. To provide the best, most persuasive answer, you usually have to clarify the objection. The good news is that the actions in Resolve will help you work through any objection, and the actions are always the same.

Once you master these actions, you will be free to draw on the appropriate technical information in the best way that can remove the objection.

Using the actions points you in the right direction and reduces pressure on you. It helps you make the most of your "answer." Equally important is that these actions help you avoid being defensive and/or exacerbating the situation with an answer that fuels the fire rather than extinguishes it. Most importantly, the actions spare you from the all but impossible task of trying to satisfy an objection that is vague.

In many ways, responding to an objection is a miniature sale. In each response you move from connecting to exploring to leveraging to checking.

Resolve is Step 4 in the sales call. Let's look inside each of the 4 Actions:

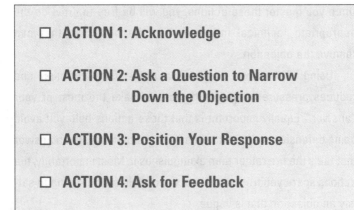

☐ **ACTION 1: Acknowledge**

☐ **ACTION 2: Ask a Question to Narrow Down the Objection**

☐ **ACTION 3: Position Your Response**

☐ **ACTION 4: Ask for Feedback**

ACTION 1: Acknowledge

If you are like most salespeople, you are eager to remove road-blocks that threaten your sale. When a customer objects, you generate adrenalin and your natural instinct often is to fight back with a quick response that, even if said politely, tells the customer why he or she is wrong. While defensiveness may be natural, it is not helpful. Responding immediately with a rebuttal invites a defensive reaction from the customer who in turn digs in his or her heels. If instead you acknowledge or empathize, you can help neutralize the situation and help lower the customer's guard.

Unfortunately, acknowledgment doesn't come naturally to most salespeople confronted by objections. Some salespeople think acknowledgment shows agreement or weakness. On the contrary, it lets the customer know you are listening, you respect his or her thinking, and that you are interested in what he or she has to say. Acknowledgment also helps you regain control. It fosters true dialogue because it helps you connect and paves the way for probing.

Acknowledgment is not agreement.
      It is neutral,
            polite,
                    and considerate.

Acknowledgment helps maintain rapport, sets you up to ask questions, and encourages your customer to provide more information. Using empathy to acknowledge objections that are personal, serious, or sensitive, is not soft. It is human. And it is appreciated by most customers.

Acknowledgment also gives you a moment to think and begin to organize your thoughts. Pausing, with a second of silence, versus giving a fast reply before beginning to respond, also shows you are thoughtful.

Whenever you are stuck,
hold back trying to answer
and acknowledge and probe.

ACTION 2: Ask a Question to Narrow Down the Objection

Since most customer objections are general in nature, your job is to narrow down the objection so it is as specific as possible. Customers say things such as: "You are not flexible," "You don't have a...," "You're not competitive," and the list goes on and on. It is important to find out more before responding to such objections. Otherwise, you will have to make assumptions about the underlying issue and maneuver in the dark. Moreover, your response probably won't address the customer's concern. Even if the basics of your answer are on the right track, without getting additional customer input, you are tasked with the job of convincing the customer versus problem-solving with them. By probing the objection, you will get the specifics you need to provide a targeted response and you will begin to help your customers change their own minds.

Ask an open-ended question to probe the objection directly. Probe the ambiguous, vague, emotional, or underscored words or phrases in the objection. Most of the time, there will be at least one, often more than one, word to query. Your job is to listen for those words so you can clarify them. For example:

- **Customer:** "You don't do X."
- **You:** "I know X is a concern. May I ask why X is important to you?" or "Why is this a concern?"

Probing is essential to clarifying objections and uncovering the needs behind them. The acknowledgment before the probe softens the question so it doesn't feel like an interrogation.

Most salespeople have a hard time asking the first question because the answers often seem too obvious. In one form or another it is a "why" question such as, "Why is X important to you?" "Why do you think we are not *flexible*?" "What makes you feel we are not *competitive*?" "In what way did our proposal miss the mark?" It may be the absolute simplicity of the question itself that is the obstacle.

The thing to remember about an objection is that, for every customer who voices the exact same objection, there are almost

114

that many different reasons driving the objection. For example, if different customers say, "We are not interested in X," each customer may have a different reason. One may have already tried it, another may have heard negative things about it in general or about your product specifically, another may question your company's commitment and long-term plans for the product, another may have no time to implement it, another may have just signed a contract for it, another may have no budget, another may prefer Y, another may have a brother-in-law in the business, and so on and so on. Probing and understanding the specifics of the objection gives you the best, if not only, chance at resolving it.

> You can't resolve
> a vague objection.

When you probe you may be surprised by how much you learn—especially if you have paved the way with acknowledgment. Customers will begin to reveal what it will take to sell them. Others may share details from a competitive proposal, pricing information, and information about decision influencers—all clues that you may never have learned without asking.

Even if you feel you know what is behind the objection and you are right, asking a question serves another important purpose—it reduces customer defensiveness and increases the customer's receptiveness to your response. The problem with thinking you have the "answer" without probing is that it may not be the answer the customer had in mind.

What's the worst that can happen? Outright refusal to answer your question. Perhaps this customer is not really a prospect. Isn't that good to know sooner rather than later? In any event, you must try to understand the customer's objections. But if customers won't provide specifics, that in itself can tell you something about the customer and how the customer views the relationship with your organization and with you.

Probing helps change an objection from a deal-stopper to a dialogue. Working with the customer, you can resolve the objection. And even when you can't, you can learn something that helps you adjust your strategy or refine your product.

If you acknowledge and probe most objections, your responses will make more sense and be more persuasive. **Rule of Thumb:** Whenever you are stuck, acknowledge what the customer has said and probe.

ACTION 3: Position Your Response

One of the best things about objections is that there are few new ones. You likely hear the same objections again and again. Even if you are a new salesperson, with training and coaching, you can be prepared with solid technical answers for the most common objections.

As mentioned previously, the problem is that it takes more than technical knowledge to satisfy customer objections. It takes dialogue.

By acknowledging

and probing,

you have shown that you have listened.

You have helped prepare the customer to listen to you. The key now is to use what you have learned to customize your response to the customer's specific concern. Leverage your technical knowledge by linking it to the concern or need you uncovered. You can incorporate the customer's exact language without sounding like a parrot. The more customers hear their concerns in your response, the more your response will resonate with them. For major objections, be ready to include a relevant example or success story to make your answers come alive. For example, if a customer tells you he is not interested in your product because of environmental concerns, once you understand those concerns, you can provide data on the safety standards that your product meets and then, to help the customer identify with the solution, add a short success story that clearly demonstrates your product's safety.

Resolve objections with your customers, not for them.

ACTION 4: Ask for Feedback

Once you have positioned your response to an objection, ask a question to determine how well your response satisfied the concern. By asking a question such as, "How does our... address the concern about...?" you can get the critical information you need that tells you how the customer feels about what you have said, where you stand, and what to do next.

Instead of asking for feedback, many salespeople respond to an objection and move on to their next point or they simply remain silent, leaving what happens next up to the customer. By not directly asking for feedback, especially if the customer doesn't offer it, you will have no way to know if you have removed the obstacle or if it is still there.

If your customer responds with a vague answer, keep probing. Acknowledge the response and ask a question to get the specifics you need. When it comes to objections, "No news is bad news," and "The least said, the slowest mended," to rewrite the old cliché.

The discipline of asking for feedback once you've presented your response will allow you to make adjustments when you need to or move forward knowing you are on solid ground. One astute sales manager said to his sales team, "Okay, I get it. We've been ending everything we say to our customers with a period. Now we've got to end everything we say with a question mark."

UNSPOKEN OBJECTIONS

When a customer does not raise an objection that your experience tells you to expect, while you don't want to introduce a negative, you can ask a neutral question that probes the issue. For example, if you anticipate resistance from local managers to a plan for centralizing operations, ask, "Bob, how do you think the district heads will respond to this plan?"

Wolf in Sheep's Clothing

Most customer questions are not objections. Many questions are just inquiries with no hidden agenda. But even "neutral" questions from customers can lead to obstacles. One salesperson faced an unexpected question at the end of a long sales cycle when a senior decision maker asked how the salesperson's solution would integrate with their new and very expensive customer management system. Without clarifying the question, the sales-

121

person gave her best answer and checked to see if her response satisfied the customer. The question turned into an objection. Her customer said, "That's very disappointing to hear. I'd think you could do more than that. We could do that."

The salesperson was struck silent for a moment, but the discipline of the steps kicked in. She acknowledged and questioned the customer to learn what he had in mind in regard to the integration. She listened and probed again. Fast on her feet, she specifically addressed his concern by adding an additional idea and detail to her initial answer. When she checked for feedback again to determine how this addressed the customer's concern, the senior said, "I feel a lot better. That's exactly what I'm looking for." Within a week, a $2.5 million contract was hers.

A response to an objection is a mini "sales call."

While most questions are not objections, sometimes customers deliver objections in the form of a question. Use your experience and intuition to help you recognize when this happens. If the question comes from a decision maker that is not supporting your solution, or if the question strikes at your key disadvantage, handle it with care and treat it like an objection. For example, if a client who has been quiet in a meeting asks as her first question, a question you have been concerned about because you realize this is a disadvantage for your company, such as "Do you have an office here?," respond by saying, "I appreciate that question. At this time we do not. We do have… and a… (describe any related advantage or upcoming plan). May I ask why you are asking about a local office?"

Then listen,
> **position your best response,**
>> **and ask for feedback on how you**
>> **addressed the question.**

Acknowledge any question that is broad and probe it to get the insight you need to respond specifically and persuasively. Use a success story if the question is pivotal. For example, at the end of a major presentation, the decision maker who had asked a number of tough questions and who had been fairly deadpan throughout the meeting, asked the salesperson to summarize

123

what it would take for the project to succeed. The salesperson not only responded to the question, but he also added a success story to illustrate how this worked for a world-class customer. When he checked for feedback the client stated she was impressed and asked if the salesperson could arrange a call with the client.

Also always be ready for questions that may be sensitive. One salesperson, a marketing consultant, lost any chance for new business because of the answer she gave to the company's president. The president, early in the meeting, handed her a small Lucite box that contained his company's vision statement. He asked her what she thought of it. Within a minute she gave a frank and harsh assessment. While it is important to be honest, it is foolish to be painfully blunt, especially when you really don't have sufficient background information. Had she said something like, "So I may give you my best assessment, may I ask a few questions? Vision has different meanings and purposes. Can you tell me what the purpose and use of this is?" she likely would have gotten some insights to let her know this was the president's handiwork and pride and joy.

Objections and questions often are vague. They can also seem challenging and stir up defensiveness. When you get an objection or a vague question, make sure you understand it and the person stating it before you answer.

Meet objections
with acknowledgment
and questions—first.

STEP FOUR: RESOLVE

☐ **ACTION 1: Acknowledge**

☐ **ACTION 2: Ask a Question to Narrow Down**
the Objection

☐ **ACTION 3: Position Your Response**

☐ **ACTION 4: Ask for Feedback**

RESOLVE PRE-CALL PLANNER

Customer: _____   *Date:* _____

Call Objective _____

Anticipated Objections	Acknowledge	Clarifying Question	Customized Response	Question to Ask for Feedback

©2008 Linda Richardson

(To access Perfect Selling tools and test please go to
http://www.richardson.com/Resource-Center/Perfect-Selling-Tools/
and enter Username: **perfectseller** and Password: **Richardson**)

127

RESOLVE POST-CALL DEBRIEF

Customer: _____ **Date:** _____

Call Objective _____

	Yes	No	Notes/Action Steps
Acknowledgment/ Empathy Statement	☐	☐	
■ Did you acknowledge the objection? ■ Did you empathize if the objections were more personal, serious, or emotional?			

	Yes	No	Notes/Action Steps
Question to Narrow Down Objection	☐	☐	
■ Did you probe to narrow the objection? ■ Did you drill down?			

	Yes	No	Notes/Action Steps
Customized Response/ Recommendation	☐	☐	
■ Did you tailor your response?			

©2008 Linda Richardson

(To access Perfect Selling tools and test please go to
http://www.richardson.com/Resource-Center/Perfect-Selling-Tools/
and enter Username: **perfectseller** and Password: **Richardson**)

128

	Yes	No	Notes/Action Steps
Customized Response/ Recommendation	☐	☐	
■ Did you incorporate your customer's language into your response? ■ Did you use a success story to further persuade the customer (optional)?			

	Yes	No	Notes/Action Steps
Check for Feedback	☐	☐	
■ Did you ask the customer for feedback to learn how your response addressed his or her objection? ■ Did you resolve the objection? ■ Did you uncover any other objections?			

©2008 Linda Richardson

■ Will you continue to work on Step 4, Resolve, or move on to Step 5, Act?

☐ Continue to work on Step 3

☐ Move to Step 4

(To access Perfect Selling tools and test please go to
http://www.richardson.com/Resource-Center/Perfect-Selling-Tools/
and enter Username: **perfectseller** and Password: **Richardson**)

FIVE

ACT

THE CLOSER

Closers are people who know how to get things done. Closers are action oriented.

It goes without saying that **the Close** is the moment in the sale when a salesperson asks for the business. Closing is a pivotal step in the sales call and sales cycle with a lot of pressure on both the salesperson and the customer. For most salespeople and customers, too, the close can seem like the moment of truth—yes or no, go or no go.

With so much at stake, many salespeople are reluctant to close. They don't want to hear a no. They don't want to risk shutting down the dialogue. They don't want to be too aggressive, too pushy. But there is a lot more at stake if they don't close with a solid, specific next step.

It is puzzling to watch some salespeople who end sales calls without meaningful action. Most of the time the salesperson has worked very hard to get time with the customer. The salesperson has worked very hard during the call to connect and persuade. Yet, when it is time to end the call, all that effort is dissipated because the salesperson doesn't ask for the business or seek agreement to a specific next step.

There are three kinds of closes:

1. **the Dotted Line Close**

   in which a salesperson asks for the business, as in, "Well, Tom, we would be honored to be your partner. We can begin immediately. Can we count on your support in moving forward?" (or "Do we have your okay?")

2. **the Momentum Close**

   in which a salesperson asks for the next step in the sales cycle, as in, "How does your calendar look for a planning session for Friday?"

3. **the "Safe" Close**

   in which a salesperson doesn't ask for anything that moves the process forward (and so avoids the chance of rejection, but loses sales momentum).

The fastest way to lose business is not to ask for it.

"Safe" closes sound like this: "Let me think about this and get back to you," "Let me contact your assistant to set up...," "Let me talk to our specialists and get back to you," "Let me write up a... and send... to you," "Let me get... to you," or "Let me follow up with an outline... proposal...," and so on.

A "safe" close can do more than delay the close. It can cost the opportunity. It often creates busy work for the salespeople and results in their spinning their wheels or wasting their team members' time. Each of these safe-close "actions" do little more than mark time. They are one-sided with the salespeople doing all the work. They lack any commitment from the customer.

While any of these three closes could be appropriate under certain circumstances, they should be the exception. The objective for the end of each call is to nail down a much more specific **next action** for the salesperson and customer such as a date and time to move forward in the next phase or milestone in the sales cycle.

A "safe" close is actually very dangerous. Once momentum is lost, reconnecting after a "safe" close can be far from easy. In fact, the safest close directly seeks a specific "next action" step with time frame, whether it is to arrange a next meeting or to ask for the customer's commitment to buy.

Of course, fear of rejection is a factor in why salespeople can be reluctant to close, but more often than not it is because they have not really defined the action step they want and lack a sales process to help them get there.

CLOSING ACTION STEPS

There are 3 actions you can take that can help turn you into a closer who closes more quickly. These actions will all but remove concerns about rejection, help you know what action you want to take, and help you in closing more business. They will help you maintain momentum and move the sale forward. The interesting thing is that only one of these three actions actually takes place in the "Act."

Thinking of the close as something that happens only in the final moments of the call is too simplistic. While the close does come at the end, it starts *before* the call, when you set your objective. It is woven through the entire call as you ask checking questions to get incremental feedback. When you do ask for the business or next step, it's less like "popping" the question and more like a joint conclusion in which your customer and you arrive at the action step together.

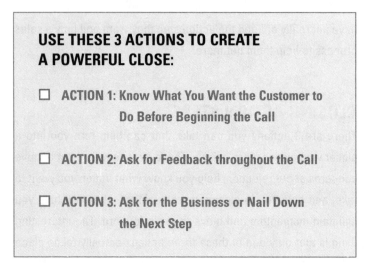

**USE THESE 3 ACTIONS TO CREATE
A POWERFUL CLOSE:**

☐ ACTION 1: Know What You Want the Customer to
            Do Before Beginning the Call

☐ ACTION 2: Ask for Feedback throughout the Call

☐ ACTION 3: Ask for the Business or Nail Down
            the Next Step

ACTION 1: Know What You Want the Customer to Do Before Beginning the Call

Far from being "all or nothing" at the end of the call, closing is a layered process that begins before the meeting with the customer starts. Before every call, define what you want to accomplish by setting a concrete, measurable call objective that clearly describes the results you want to see at the end of the call. When you walk out of the sales call you should be able to answer the question, "Did I do X or not?" and get a very clear answer.

Objectives such as, "Better understand the customer's needs," or "Learn more about the customer's priorities" are commendable, but they are not concrete or measurable. However, specific actions, such as, "Get a copy of the customer's portfolio and set a meeting to get together again within 10 days," "Get a list of the criteria the customer will use to make a decision and gain agreement to accept a proposal by...," or "Gain agreement today to move forward on..." can be clearly measured—yes, you did it or no, you did not. Not only will this help you close more sales, it will give you a reality check on where you are with this customer.

The objective you set for each call should be aggressive yet appropriate for where you are in the sales cycle. For example, it would be unreasonable to expect to gain commitment for a complex purchase on the first call with a prospect. But you can accelerate getting that go-ahead from the customer if before each call you clearly define the next action step you want that will take you forward. Make it your plan to leave the call with the appropriate next step in place, whether it is to set the date for a demo, bring in a specialist, or get the handshake or signature that seals the deal.

Know what you want
and ask for it.

ACTION 2: Ask for Feedback throughout the Call

No one likes rejection. If, however, you can reasonably predict how the customer will respond to your asking for the next step or for the business, you can be more confident and lower your chance of rejection. Asking checking questions to get feedback throughout the call is a way to do this. Customer feedback will let you know how your customer feels and thinks about what you have presented. Asking for feedback is technically not a part of Step 5 since this action takes place throughout the call—Steps 1, 2, 3, 4, and 5. You are literally weaving your way to the close sharing in Connect when you check how your agenda meets the customer's expectations. Checking for feedback throughout the call serves as a thread "to sew up the deal" and gives you the knowledge and confidence to ask for action at the end of the call.

Some sales professionals have an acute level of awareness, whether natural or honed, that registers the slightest customer reaction or shift. But most of us need something more concrete to alert us to how the customer feels—checking is just that.

> By asking questions such as,
> "How does that sound?"
> "What do you think?"
> or
> "How would
> that work?"

every time you position your capabilities or respond to an objection or question, you learn what your customer thinks about what you have said to help you move closer to closing. For example, if you describe something about your product, and then ask, "How would this work with your multiple sites?" you will get the feedback that will let you know where you stand relative to closing. If you wait until the end of the call to find this out, you probably won't have time to make any adjustments that are needed.

Checking serves as the buildup to your bottom line or momentum close. Just before you are about to ask for the next step or the business, ask your final checking question to determine how the customer feels about the recommendation or ideas you have presented.

When your customer responds positively to your checking questions and, in particular, your final checking question in which you ask how your solution meets the customer's needs, you get the data and encouragement you need to ask confidently for the next step or the business. If the feedback is sparse or negative, you can probe more, reposition, make a second effort, and, if necessary, adjust your solution or objective. By asking for feedback throughout the call, you are preparing yourself and your customer to move forward. You reduce any concerns associated with closing because you can fairly certainly predict the customer's response—**your customer has been primed.**

ACTION 3: Ask for the Business or Nail Down the Next Step

At the end of the call, the choice is yours. You can maintain momentum or lose it. You can move ahead or stand still (while competitors may be charging ahead). When you confidently ask for the business or arrange the specific next step so that it is firmly in place, you are poised to move forward before you walk out the door or hang up the phone. Whatever you do, don't assume your customer isn't ready to take the next step or make a decision.

Initiate a **bottom line close** by saying:

- "We can begin tomorrow. All I need is your go-ahead."
- "Our team is ready. We very much want to support you in... Can we move forward on this?"
- "You can begin to... Do I have your go-ahead?"

Or, for a **momentum close**:

■ "Since you want to… we can… next week, to make sure this is a good match for you. We discussed the role of your district heads. How do you feel about my meeting with them to discuss… (benefit) over the next week to get their input? I can get back to you with our findings early the following week. How is that? … I have the three names of the district heads you mentioned. Are there any others I should contact? … Will you let them know I'll be calling? Thanks. What should I know about them so I am prepared? … Shall we take out our calendar and pencil in our follow-up meeting the week of…?"

Practice asking for things.

Once you get agreement, be specific—nail down the next steps of who, when, where, to get started.

If, when you ask for your action step, your customer does not agree despite having given positive feedback throughout the call, you are on solid ground to acknowledge the customer's feelings and nondefensively probe the reason, to address it, make a second effort, or adjust your objective.

In situations in which you are not sure of the next step, at a minimum ask the customer, "What do you see as the next step?" But don't settle for a "Let me think about it and get back to you." If the customer suggests getting back to you, say, "Great. May I call you on... (date) to...?" and ask for a reasonable next step that is in your control, not the customer's. When you walk out the door, be in the driver's seat!

Regardless of where you are in the sales cycle, at the end of each contact plant the seed for closing and winning the business by telling the customer how much you would like to work with him or her. For example, "Paul, your... sounds... (compliment the customer) and this is an area where we... (tout your expertise)... It really would be a privilege to work with you. I hope we can partner (work) with you on this."

PS: LAST IMPRESSION

Right before you leave, take a moment to personalize the good-by as a way to leave the best impression. Say thank you and reference something personal that you may have learned as you prepared or during the dialogue such as, "Good luck with the tournament." "Enjoy the concert."

Everyone loves a closer.

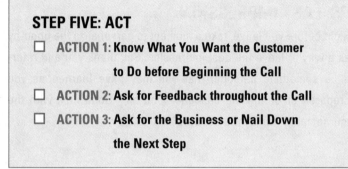

STEP FIVE: ACT

☐ ACTION 1: Know What You Want the Customer
to Do before Beginning the Call

☐ ACTION 2: Ask for Feedback throughout the Call

☐ ACTION 3: Ask for the Business or Nail Down
the Next Step

ACT PRE-CALL PLANNER

Customer: _____ **Date:** _____

Call Objective _____

☐ Bottom Line Close   ☐ Momentum Close

Know What You Want the Customer to Do
(Set a Measurable Objective)

Checking Questions
(At what key points in the dialogue will you ask for feedback?)

Ask for Business or Next Step

Leave a Positive Last Impression:

(To access Perfect Selling tools and test please go to
http://www.richardson.com/Resource-Center/Perfect-Selling-Tools/
and enter Username: **perfectseller** and Password: **Richardson**)

ACT POST-CALL DEBRIEF

Customer: _____ **Date:** _____

Call Objective _____

	Yes	No	Notes/Action Steps
Did You Set a Measurable Objective?	☐	☐	
■ Did I set a measurable objective with a time frame?			

	Yes	No	Notes/Action Steps
Checking Questions (Ask for Feedback throughout Call)	☐	☐	
■ Did I ask for feedback throughout the call to guide the customer's response?			

	Yes	No	Notes/Action Steps
Ask for Business or Next Step (Always Plant the Seed)	☐	☐	
■ Did I ask for the business or the specific next step?			
■ Did I achieve my objective?			

(To access Perfect Selling tools and test please go to
http://www.richardson.com/Resource-Center/Perfect-Selling-Tools/
and enter Username: **perfectseller** and Password: **Richardson**)

	Yes	No	Notes/Action Steps
Positive Last Impression	☐	☐	
■ Did I leave a positive last impression?			

■ Will you continue to work on Step 5, Act?

☐ Continue to work on Step 5

©2008 Linda Richardson

(To access Perfect Selling tools and test please go to
http://www.richardson.com/Resource-Center/Perfect-Selling-Tools/
and enter Username: **perfectseller** and Password: **Richardson**)

149

5
steps
to

extraordinary
but fast
preparation

While the sales call itself is a gold mine for identifying needs, what you know about your prospects and customers before you go to the call is essential to making the most of the 5 Steps. In addition to setting your call objective and doing traditional homework, you can now leverage the Web to gain insight into how your prospect or customer views itself as an organization and tap into your network.

Today, the Web has made organizational and individual prospect and customer research fast and easy and networking as accessible as never before.

> At a minimum, go to your customers' Web site.
>> Learn about the organization and
>> its executives.
> What challenges are they facing?
>> Take a look at the language they
>> use to describe themselves.
>>> Do they see themselves
>>> as innovators?
> Are they proud of their history,
> their team orientation, their founder?
>> What key phrases do they use to
>> describe themselves?

152

Create a list of **key phrases** or words. Ask yourself what this information means and how you can use it to supplement what you learn in your customer dialogue and other homework to make what you present as persuasive as possible. Review your notes from your customer information management system. Tap into your team resources. And check out your competitors' Web sites as well as industry associations.

Start with customer preparation to shorten your preparation time and be more strategic in your technical preparation. Use the 5 Steps to help you prepare for each call.

To help you prepare quickly, walk through the 5 Steps and Actions:

STEP 1: CONNECT

- How will you build rapport? Personal? Business?
- What has led to this call? What has transpired up to now? How will you get credit for your homework?
- How will you introduce your organization and self if needed?

STEP 2: EXPLORE

- What questions will you ask?
- Have you included strategic as well as technical questions?
- What questions are the customers likely to ask?

STEP 3: LEVERAGE

- What will you present?
- How can you customize this to the customer's needs?
- What alternatives are you preparing?
- What materials do you need to support you?
- What success story or example are you prepared to give?

STEP 4 : RESOLVE

- What objections do you anticipate?
- How will you resolve them?

STEP 5: ACT

- Did you achieve your measurable objective for this call?
- How will you end the call?
- What is the specific action step/time frame you will seek?

The temptation to wing sales calls can be great, especially if you are experienced or if you face customer demands, administrative tasks, and all the other pressures of the job. Even so, to maximize every customer contact, preparation is mandatory. It not only leads to more successful calls, it changes how you present yourself. You know when you are prepared and that helps you project confidence.

While customers *may* not *always* know when you are *not* prepared, there is no question that they do know when you are.

> Preparation leads to
> points earned, respect,
> and more business.

POST-CALL SMALL DOSE DEBRIEF

While you are probably supported by a team, it is likely that you are making the majority of your sales calls by yourself. When you will have no colleague to share his or her perspective of the customer's needs and your sales performance, it is all the more important to you to self-assess after the call. You can use the 5 Steps to self-coach every day to reap the power of incremental growth. By taking a few minutes to reflect on your calls, you will increase self-awareness and continuously improve.

You may think you don't have the time to debrief after your sales calls. It is true many sales calls are back-to-back, there are challenges with travel, and cell phones and handhelds require attention between calls. More often than not, however, the real culprit for not debriefing calls is just not thinking to do it—or not even knowing to do it. If you are like most salespeople, you haven't had role models for whom debriefing calls was a sales discipline. Even well-meaning, committed sales managers can fall back on comments like, "Good call" as the call debrief versus talking about what made it a good call and what could make it better next time.

Of course, you think about what you have to do to follow up on a call and, as critical as that is, follow-up won't necessarily make you better. Not many salespeople truly stop and reflect on how they led the call versus exclusively thinking about what was accomplished and what needs to be done next.

The opportunity for continuous improvement is there for the taking and it takes only a few minutes. It is almost guaranteed to make your next call more successful. The requirement is a commitment to set aside a *few minutes immediately after* each call to look honestly at the call from not only a results perspective but call leadership perspective. Debriefing does not have to be laborious or academic. Salespeople who are good at this can literally debrief a call in a few minutes.

How to Debrief a Call

The purpose for debriefing a call is improvement through assessment and correction. To do this, think through the 5 Steps:

- **Connect:** Presence, rapport, leverage preparation, transition to needs.
- **Explore:** Probing for needs, drilling down.
- **Leverage:** Structuring, customizing, customizing, customizing, checking.
- **Resolve:** Clarify and address specific objections. Check for feedback.

and

- **Act:** Objective achieved, clear specific next step set.

As you think through the 5 Steps, first, identify what went well. Then, focus on what could have been improved. Initially, you can use either the debriefing tool for each Step (if you are focusing on one Step) or the Sales Call Debriefing tool on page 160, or just mentally walk through the 5 Steps.

As you debrief the call be sure not to ignore your strengths. You can learn so much from them and you deserve the pat on the back. But don't ignore where you dropped the ball either. Identify:

ONE key strength
and
ONE key area for improvement.

157

For example, one salesperson realized her effectiveness at questioning was slipping. The client asked two questions, which she answered, but after the call, as she debriefed, she realized she never got feedback or even clarified why the customer cared about the issues. So for her next call, questioning and listening were high on her radar screen.

Once you have identified one area to work on, compare it to trends in past calls to gain more insight. Set a plan for corrective action, whether it is to enhance your product knowledge, focus on questioning on your next call, or ending the next call with a specific action step in place.

Debriefing the call also helps you identify additional action steps beyond the ones you have committed to. For example, if you hadn't ended on a specific action step, you could send a follow-up e-mail or make a phone call to regain momentum by suggesting a follow-up date.

Debriefing can also help you populate your customer relationship management system with more than numbers and technical facts. Include insights, customer language, concerns, personal data such as birthday dates—all the information you can use for follow-up, to prepare for your next contact, and differentiate yourself.

TEAM CALL DEBRIEF

When you are on a team call with a colleague, debriefing can be equally effective and fast. Agree before the sales call to debrief the call for a few minutes (maximum eight minutes and as short as two minutes). Commit to listen to one another's feedback without offering excuses or becoming defensive. To facilitate a team call debrief, begin with an assessment of your own performance. Identify one area of strength and one area of improvement (two at the most). Be specific. Use examples.

- Then ask your colleague to give you feedback—also one key strength and area for improvement.
- Your colleague should then repeat the process.
- Discuss your teamwork and how you supported one another.
- Each of you should decide on something to work on in future calls and something to work on to improve teamwork.

Of course, assess how well you achieved the objective of the call and focus on your follow-up. But also take a few moments to consider how well you teamed. Become your own and each other's coach.

SALES CALL DEBRIEF

Customer: _____ *Date:* _____

Call Objective _____

	Yes	No	Notes/Action Steps
CONNECT	☐	☐	
Personal/Business Rapport			
Summary of Events			
Leverage Preparation			
Dual Purpose			
Transition to Needs			

	Yes	No	Notes/Action Steps
EXPLORE	☐	☐	
Customer Objectives			
Current Situation			
Technical Needs			
Future Needs			
Personal Drivers			

©2008 Linda Richardson

(To access Perfect Selling tools and test please go to
http://www.richardson.com/Resource-Center/Perfect-Selling-Tools/
and enter Username: **perfectseller** and Password: **Richardson**)

	Yes	No	Notes/Action Steps
LEVERAGE	☐	☐	
Introduce Solution			
Customize Solution			
Summarize			

	Yes	No	Notes/Action Steps
RESOLVE	☐	☐	
Acknowledge/Empathy			
Clarify			
Customize Response/ Recommendation			
Check for Feedback			

	Yes	No	Notes/Action Steps
ACT	☐	☐	
Set a Measurable Objective before Call			
Ask Checking Questions throughout the Call			
Ask for Business or Next Step			
Leave Positive Last Impression			

©2008 Linda Richardson

(To access Perfect Selling tools and test please go to
http://www.richardson.com/Resource-Center/Perfect-Selling-Tools/
and enter Username: **perfectseller** and Password: **Richardson**)

your

plan

ONE STEP AT A TIME

Start by working on the 5 Steps in sequence one at a time, Monday through Friday (or one a week, or whatever works for you). Your goal is to make each Step second nature to you.

Read the Step and study the Actions. Before your calls, use the Planner to prepare and then focus on that Step for the day (or week) as you make your sales calls. At the end of the day use the call Post-Call Debrief for that Step to assess your results and self-coach. Once the Step is mastered move on to the next Step.

Tap into as many resources as you can to strengthen your sales performance. Just as a top athlete has more than one coach—you can also have multiple coaches:

- Ask your manager for coaching and feedback.
- Ask your colleagues for feedback. Make a pact with them to coach one another.
- Self-coach every day by debriefing your calls, not only for call outcome and follow-up, but for how you lead the call using the 5 Steps.

Use all available resources, such as:

- Richardson Cyber Sales and Manager Tips™, which are complimentary monthly Web-based tips for salespeople on topics such as selling, negotiating, prospecting...available through www.richardson.com and Ask Richardson—24-hour turnaround complimentary service for answering your sales and sales management questions
- Sales books, CDs, sales magazines such as Selling Power
- Seminars, Webinars, podcasts, blogs
- Perfect Selling tools, which can be accessed by visiting http://www.richardson.com/Resource-Center/Perfect-Selling-Tools/ and enter Username: perfectseller and Password: Richardson
- Internet research on customers, industries, competitors

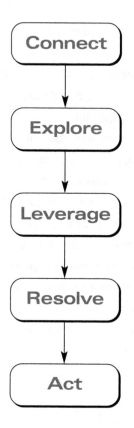

You are in sales because you belong in sales.

It is the path you have found (or has found you) and the path you are on. And because the sales call is the road you travel, the more you know about it, the more control you will have over how you move through each call, and the more successful you will be. Mastering the 5 Steps will improve your dialogues, making them more interactive, more organized, and more rewarding for your customers and you. It will help you put your customers first. It will help you become first with your customers. It will help you gain new customers and expand present ones.

You have what it takes for perfect selling every time. Dialogue is the tool of your trade. Dialogue is what your customers do to let you into their world. Dialogue is what you use to shape your customers' perceptions of you and the value you bring.

The minute you are face to face with your customer, it's time to be your best. By knowing the 5 Steps of a sales call so they are second nature to you, you will be able to guide yourself through each sales call. With the 5 Steps under your cap, you will direct the dialogue to lead it to where you want it to go. Once the Steps are second nature to you, you will still think about them, but the element of technicality will disappear.

The 5 Steps of a sales call are the mechanics. Your execution is the art. If you are experienced in sales, you know your next level of sales excellence is one step in front of you. If you are just beginning to shape your selling universe, you have an exciting journey before you.

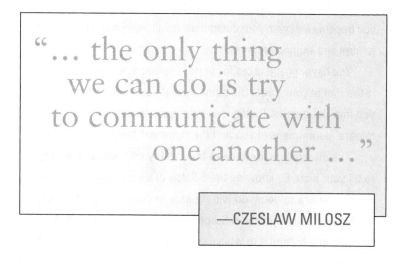

"... the only thing we can do is try to communicate with one another ..."

—CZESLAW MILOSZ

Mastering the 5 Steps frees you to:

- Pay close attention to the level of relationships you have with your customers.
- Ask more questions and listen actively.
- Know how your customers think and feel.
- Talk your customer's language.
- Increase how persuasive you are.
- Truly add value.
- Build and deepen customer relationships.
- Win more business.

Perfect Selling is a process. It requires seeking and gaining self-knowledge. By taking the time to learn the 5 Steps, by applying them one at a time and being committed to self-coaching, you will perfect your selling. You'll begin to think, "It's too easy" because you will know what to do in each sales call to win and you will do just that—call after call.

And that defines Perfect Selling.

About the Author

Linda Richardson is the founder and executive chairwoman of Richardson, a global sales training business. As a recognized leader in the industry, she has won the coveted Stevie Award for Lifetime Achievement in Sales Excellence for 2006, and in 2007 she was identified by Training Industry, Inc. as  one of the "Top 20 Most Influential Training Professionals."

Linda is the author of nine books on selling and sales management, including her most recent works, *The Sales Success Handbook*, *Sales Coaching*, and *Stop Telling, Start Selling*. She has been published extensively in industry and training journals and has been featured in numerous publications, including the *Wall Street Journal*, *Forbes*, *Nation's Business*, *Selling Power*, *Success*, and *The Conference Board Magazine*.

Linda teaches sales and management courses at the Wharton Graduate School of the University of Pennsylvania and the Wharton Executive Development Center. She is a frequent speaker at industry and client conferences.

Dialogue.
Knowledge.
Network.
Tools.

Results.

Selling in a 2.0 World

How Customers Buy Has *Really* Changed!

Dialogue is at the heart of all we do! Richardson's focus has always been on helping salespeople succeed. Our sales, service, and sales management training solutions have changed the way hundreds of thousands of sales professionals engage their customers, understand customer drivers for success, and achieve results. Our solutions continue to change to align with how customers buy and leverage the tools available to customers and sales teams.

In the class, on the Web, or in the field, Richardson has the processes, methodology and tools needed for success in a 2.0 world.

Learn More Today

For more information about Richardson's training solutions, please contact us at 800.526.1650 or visit us on the Web at **www.richardson.com**.

R RICHARDSON
THE POWER TO SELL